The 5-Ingredient
Fresh & Easy cookbook

THE
5-Ingredient
Fresh & Easy
cookbook

90+ recipes for busy people
who love to eat well

SHEILA THIGPEN

**ROCKRIDGE
PRESS**

Interior & Cover Designer: Jami Spittler
Art Producer: Maura Boland
Editor: Natasha Yglesias
Production Editor: Matt Burnett

Photography © Monica Buck, Food styling by Stacey Stolman; © Darren Muir, p. vi; © Nadine Greef, p. x; © Marija Vidal, p. 160. Author photo courtesy of © Brittany Miller Photography

Cover: Veggie Frittata, page 32

ISBN: Print 978-1-64611-003-2 | eBook 978-1-64611-004-9

To John, my husband, best friend, and constant encourager; my daughters, Allison and Lindsay, who always cheer me on; and sweet Jyothika, who brings me joy.

Contents

Introduction

I get it. You love to eat well and want to feel good (maybe even a little proud) when you call friends and family to the table. But life just keeps happening, and modern routines don't always help the home chef.

If you're in what I'd call a high-hustle phase of life—juggling your career, shuttling kids, commuting to work, or just trying to rally your friends for dinner despite everyone's busy schedules—I'm glad you picked up this book.

I adore cooking and come from a long line of Southern farm-to-table cooks. But the women who raised me and sparked my love of great food also lived a completely different lifestyle than many of us do now. I yearned to keep those traditions alive and translate them into my crazy, but wonderful, modern life as the working mom of two amazing, oh-so-busy daughters.

For twenty years, I had a full-time publishing career while raising my kids. We all bounced between piano and violin lessons, swim team, soccer, basketball, band, orchestra, and church activities. I even got talked into coaching basketball one season!

Catching up with my girls and husband around our dinner table was the highlight of my day, so dinner needed to become a priority. But how? At first, I felt completely overwhelmed.

Unfortunately, during my early years as the family chef—long before I became a food blogger—I didn't always have a weekly meal plan. I'd find myself foraging in the pantry at the last minute, scrambling to pull together a dinner with a bit of this and dash of that.

Eventually, I realized that I needed a little planning, better organization, and *easier* recipes. When I was a teenager, my grandmother lived with us and taught me to cook delicious Southern dishes using produce from my dad's farm. Every day, she would whip up a full meal that always included fresh garden vegetables like green beans, okra, or corn, accompanied by a skillet of hot cornbread and a plate of delicious, home-grown tomatoes. At the time, I took for granted our farm-to-table lifestyle, the amazing freshness of our food, and how easily it had come together.

As an adult, my cooking evolved to include recipes from my vast cookbook collection and those I created from my own pantry challenges during the early years raising our family. What I learned was that you don't need a lot of extra ingredients to make great food. In fact, all the recipes in *The 5-Ingredient Fresh & Easy Cookbook* include just five main ingredients. I truly believe enjoying fresh, high quality, and tasty meals around your table is possible, even when you're busy. In fact, when life demands more of us, our time at the table is that much more important; it becomes a significant, restorative element in our day.

Cliché as it may sound, the kitchen really has always been the heart of our home. Not only has our kitchen table been the meeting place for our family meals, it's been the central hub for school projects, Easter egg dyeing, Christmas cookie decorating, and drop-in friends. Over the years our kitchen walls absorbed little-girl giggles, excited after-school chatter, teenage tears, and dance grooves, all while I cooked dinner. Now, when our grown-up daughters come to visit, we gather around the table for a meal and lively conversation. It's still the best part of my day.

That's how I came to understand that even in the busyness of life, it's possible to cook great meals without skimping on flavor, nutrition, or freshness. If a loaded schedule has been coming between you and eating the great meals you deserve, let's dive in and fix that!

Inside this book, you'll find useful tips to optimize your kitchen, stock your pantry, and shop smart so you can start enjoying more delicious meals while making memories around your family's table.

Happy cooking!

CHAPTER ONE

No-Fuss Deliciousness

Easy recipes are about getting back to basics. All the recipes in this cookbook are made from scratch and don't use a lot of heavy, processed, or sugary ingredients (with the exception of sweet desserts). Instead, the recipes focus on getting maximum flavor from fresh, wholesome, easy-to-find ingredients, including strategic pantry staples—all with minimum fuss.

Whether you're a seasoned cook or just starting out, this cookbook will give you clear, simple instructions and tips with every recipe to help you make meals the easy way, even when life is busy. Take it from a former project manager: The key to success with any project—even cooking—is starting with a good plan. In this chapter, I'll help you get your pantry organized, do some clever meal planning, and shop smart so you can enjoy stress-free cooking all the time. Get ready to make something delicious!

About the Recipes

I developed these recipes for busy people, pressed for time and energy, who want to make great tasting food. The recipes are delicious, nutritious, simple to prepare, and include just five main ingredients (not counting seasoning and standard flavor enhancers or herbs). Each recipe makes four to six servings with the exception of sauces and dressings, which have a greater yield.

With your cooking success in mind, many recipes also include tips for substitutions or working with a specific ingredient, flavor swaps, and other helpful shortcuts and cooking hacks.

To help make cooking and planning menus easier, the recipes are grouped into breakfast, lunch, dinner, snacks, and dessert chapters. Within each chapter, recipes are further categorized with labels indicating whether the recipe is a one-pot creation, make-ahead, no-cook, an easy classic, or a reinvention (repurposing a leftover dish or part of a dish to make something new). Let's learn more about the recipe labels together.

The Recipe Labels

One-Pot: Weeknight dinners don't get any easier than preparing a one-pot recipe like a hearty stew, comforting casserole, or simple sheet pan dinner. Add a side salad and whole-grain dinner rolls to complete the menu if you like, but, frankly, everything for a nutritious meal is in the one main dish. These recipes cook in a single pot, baking dish, or sheet pan, and some include tips for using a slow cooker instead. As an added bonus, one-pot meals also minimize cleanup!

Make-Ahead: Get a jump start on dinner with make-ahead recipes, which are prepped and stored in the fridge to be baked, cooked, or reheated later. Some of these recipes will also include freezing instructions. They are particularly handy when you are planning to feed overnight (or unexpected) guests. In these cases, a make-ahead recipe ensures you can spend more time visiting and less time cooking.

No-Cook: Forget the stove! The no-cook recipes include delicious salads and wraps made with fresh ingredients, along with quick breakfast smoothies, snacks and dips, and even some scrumptious no-bake desserts that taste good and won't leave you working up a sweat. They are fantastic to use in the summer when no one wants to turn on their stove or oven.

Easy Classic: In this cookbook, you'll find simplified versions of family favorites including pasta dishes and stir-fry creations, as well as familiar comfort foods like Sunday Roast Chicken (see page 85) and Slow Cooker Beef Pot Roast with Mushrooms (see page 83). These recipes encourage gathering around the table to savor every bite while enjoying good conversation.

Reinvention: Turn a leftover dish into something new the next night or for lunch the next day. Reinvention recipes use a leftover ingredient, such as a sauce, to help make a new recipe. Original recipes in this book will include a special footnote and reference the page number for a new recipe when you can use leftovers for another dish. These are perfect for making sure that nothing that you make goes to waste.

Where appropriate, some recipes will also include other labels indicating that they are:

* Nut-Free
* Gluten-Free
* Dairy-Free
* Soy-Free
* Vegetarian
* Vegan

For my gluten-free recipes: Please read the packaging of all the ingredients you purchase, especially oats, to make sure they were processed in a completely gluten-free facility.

Dial in Your Kitchen

One thing that stresses me out more than anything else is built-up, unnecessary clutter around the house. I'm not quite as extreme as Marie Kondo, but my family will tell you I've been known to turn into the Tasmanian Devil, speeding like a bullet, picking up and tossing out stray paraphernalia when clutter starts to creep into my home. What's frustrating is that I could avoid this if only I'd put things in their proper place along the way. Mama always said, "Put things back where they belong," and that was solid advice. It's so much easier to find what you need quickly when you need it when it's in its proper place.

The same goes for the kitchen. Keeping a tidy, organized kitchen with some open workspace is the first step toward preparing no-stress meals. I'll show you a few tricks to help you make your cooking space more usable and calming.

Declutter and Organize

Think about your pantry like a grocery shelf: sort items into like groups so you can spot them quickly and make cooking easier. For example, canned goods like beans or tomatoes could go on one shelf while baking supplies like flour and sugar could go on another. You may wish to organize your pantry shelves into these groups:

* Canned goods
* Baking supplies
* Oils and vinegars
* Grains and pastas
* Condiments
* Spices and extracts

As you sort your pantry, be sure to check the expiration dates and identify duplicate items to ensure everything warrants keeping. For example, you may be surprised to find three unopened bottles of dried oregano! By keeping your space organized, you won't purchase products you already have at home anymore.

Labels and storage tools help keep it all together: Once your pantry is decluttered, you may want to store similar items in baskets or bins. Adding labels (like "Oils and Vinegars") to the face of the shelf or storage basket will help keep it organized for the long-term. Labels also remind everyone in the household to return items to their proper place. When you restock the pantry, another good rule to follow is "first in, first out," meaning if you purchase a new jar of artichoke hearts, move the old jar to the front so it's used first.

When in doubt, throw it out: Next, look at your refrigerator and freezer in the same manner. Toss any out-of-date condiments or salad dressings to make room for fresher ingredients. Group similar items on the proper shelves, keeping the ones you use most frequently in the front. Most new refrigerators have adjustable shelves and drawers, so take the time to set them to work with the ingredients and brands you most often buy. Veggies and meats should always be stored separately to avoid cross-contamination. Usually, the meat drawer is located in the bottom of the refrigerator, and vegetable crisper bins have humidity adjustments to keep vegetables fresher longer.

Every good cook needs some elbow room: Make sure you have a nice, open work surface for preparing food and move as many items as possible off counter-tops and into storage spaces. Keep out only what you need that day. Remember Mama's advice and put things where they belong. You'll enjoy cooking so much more when you give yourself a bit of space and order.

Tune Up Your Tools

While we're at it, let's look inside those kitchen drawers. Do you really need that rusty spatula? Now is a good time to review all of your kitchen tools to ensure everything is in working order. Say goodbye to dull peelers, worn-out towels, ripped oven mitts, and especially scratched up nonstick pans that could be releasing harmful chemicals into your food. If you don't own a set of stainless-steel cookware, you might consider investing in one (see "Nonstick Cooking with Stainless Steel" on page 8 for more information).

Make sure your kitchen gear can be reached easily: Like the pantry, keep spatulas, wire whisks, and measuring spoons organized in a specific drawer. You may want to place your most used utensils in a container on one side of the countertop for easy access. Other gear, like bakeware and cookware, should be stored together in convenient cabinets near the stove. I promise these arrangements are worth the effort. You'll enjoy cooking so much more when you can find everything you need and flow through your tasks.

Stock your kitchen with the right equipment: Here is a list of the kitchen tools I find most useful for everyday cooking.

* **Measuring cups and measuring spoons:** It doesn't always work to "eyeball" measurements, especially in baking. At a minimum, I recommend a 2-cup glass measuring cup for liquids, a set of standard measuring cups for dry ingredients, and a set of measuring spoons for spices, leavening, and extracts.

* **Mixing bowls:** A set of nesting bowls in different sizes comes in handy when mixing up sauces and batters.

* **Large cutting board with a non-slip mat:** If your cutting board doesn't have a non-slip mat, always place it on a kitchen towel to stabilize it when chopping vegetables or herbs.

* **Chef's knife and small paring knife:** I use my chef's knife 80 percent of the time when cutting and preparing my food. For smaller things, like mushrooms or strawberries, I prefer a paring knife.

* **Vegetable peeler:** My favorite peeler for potatoes and carrots is the OXO Good Grips Vegetable Peeler.

* **Wire whisk:** This tool is essential for making vinaigrettes with oil and vinegar.

* **Wooden spoons:** These spoons are nonabrasive and will last forever as long as you don't leave them in a pan of water in the sink or put them in the dishwasher.

* **Tongs and turners:** Tongs with long handles are best for flipping hot items in a skillet or roasting pan and help protect you from burning your fingers.

* **Microplane zester:** This is not an essential tool, but it is one I use almost every day. I love adding lemon and orange zest to salad dressings and baking recipes.

* **Colander and salad spinner:** Salad greens will last longer if they are properly washed and dried, and a salad spinner is just the gadget for this task.

* **Saucepans:** Ideally, you should have at least two sizes—a smaller one for sauces and a larger one for boiling vegetables.

* **Frying pans:** Having at least two sizes of these is ideal as well—one 10-inch and a deep 12-inch pan are both useful.

* **Glass baking dishes:** A 9-by-13-inch baking dish is the perfect size for casseroles, enchiladas, and lasagna.

* **Cast-iron skillet:** A cast-iron skillet is a great tool for baking cornbread and searing meats.

* **Mixer:** My favorite kitchen appliance is my KitchenAid stand mixer. I even use it to shred chicken for salads!

* **Sheet pans:** Sheet pans are not only for cookies. I use mine for roasting vegetables and even cooking an entire sheet pan dinner.

* **Muffin pan:** Definitely go with a nonstick 12-cup muffin pan.

* **Slow cooker and Dutch oven:** A covered Dutch oven is my go-to pot for roasting a whole chicken or making hearty stews in the oven, but a slow cooker is awesome for fix-it-and-forget-it recipes.

* **Pasta or stock pot:** A deep pot is the most efficient way to cook pastas.

* **Food processor or blender:** Either is nice to have, especially for smoothies and shakes.

Nonstick Cooking with Stainless Steel

Nonstick pans wear out quickly, but stainless-steel pans can last for years. You can turn a stainless-steel pan into a nonstick pan with a simple, two-step technique:

1. Heat the stainless-steel pan over medium to medium high heat for a couple of minutes. Add a tablespoon of coconut oil to the pan and let it melt. Swirl the pan around to coat it all over with the melted coconut oil until the oil smokes.
2. Immediately turn off the heat and remove the pan to let it cool completely. Once completely cooled, discard the oil and wipe the pan with a paper towel. The next time you cook, the pan will work just like a nonstick pan.

As long as you don't use soap on your pan, your pan will remain nonstick. If you are using higher heat, you might need to add a little bit of oil.

Edible Essentials

Congratulations on your kitchen organization so far! Now that everything is sorted and labeled, let's talk about stocking the pantry. Don't worry, there are no specialty items on this list. This book is all about getting back to the basics without sacrificing flavor. Use this list to determine what you may want to purchase to complete your pantry and start making delicious food in your kitchen. Later, we'll discuss tips for shopping smart.

Fresh Meats

This list will vary depending on your meal plan for the week, but I typically purchase at least three of the following fresh meats weekly:

* Boneless chicken breast
* Fish or seafood
* Ground beef or roast
* Pork loin or chops
* Bacon or sausage (for weekend breakfasts)

If there's a good sale at the meat counter, I'll purchase double what I need and freeze the extra. However, I don't like having to thaw meats when I'm ready to cook, so I prefer buying fresh.

Vegetables and Fruit

When it comes to produce, I recommend shopping for fresh, local, seasonal vegetables and fruits as much as possible. Produce that has been shipped to you from far away generally doesn't have as much flavor as something that was picked recently on a nearby farm. Here are some of my favorites:

* Lemons, limes, oranges: For drinks, infused water, vinaigrettes, and baking
* Garlic, onions, peppers: These three ingredients add *so* much flavor to many other foods.
* Sweet potatoes: A baked sweet potato is an easy side to any dinner. If you don't load it up with brown sugar, it's healthier than a baked white potato.
* Salad greens: A quick salad balances out any meal
* Raw vegetables: For snacking on alone or with a tasty dip
* Other veggies: Whatever is needed for your meal plan that week
* Other fruit: For breakfast and snacks: I always try to have a few of my favorites on hand.

Fresh Herbs

Whenever possible, I prefer cooking with fresh herbs. Prepping freshly minced herbs for recipes is pure aroma therapy! When purchasing fresh herbs, be sure to store them properly so you can enjoy them throughout the week (see "Keeping Fresh Herbs Fresh" on page 14 for more information).

My favorite herbs to buy fresh are:

* Italian flat-leaf parsley
* Basil
* Cilantro
* Rosemary
* Thyme

Fridge Staples

Other than basic condiments, these are fresh items I like to keep on hand:

* Milk
* Large eggs
* Butter
* Cheese: Parmesan, feta, mozzarella, Cheddar, low-fat cream cheese
* Yogurt: Greek, preferably
* Low-fat sour cream
* Orange or apple juice

Freezer Basics

For the freezer, I mainly stock fruit for smoothies and vegetables for soups and casseroles. Freezer basics are also great when I'm running short on prep time.

* Mango or pineapple chunks
* Peaches
* Blackberries or blueberries
* Diced onions and bell peppers
* Corn, peas, or lima beans
* Edamame: These are great for snacking!
* Bread dough or whole-grain dinner rolls: This is the easiest way to enjoy fresh yeast rolls without making the dough from scratch.

Canned and Jarred Foods

The goal of this cookbook is to help guide you toward making fresh *and* easy recipes. To that end, there are certain canned and jarred foods that will help reduce effort—for example, using canned beans instead of soaking and cooking dried beans from scratch—and will also enhance the flavor of other fresh foods. In addition, there are some foods that are only in season for a short time, like really *good* tomatoes, so the canned varieties come in handy when you would like them all year round.

* Tomatoes: Whole, crushed, and diced
* Tomato paste
* Beans: Black, cannellini or white beans, plus pinto or red kidney beans for chili

* Chickpeas
* Sundried tomatoes
* Artichoke hearts
* Tuna fish
* Low-sodium chicken and beef broths or stock
* Olives: Kalamata, black, and green
* Pimentos
* Capers
* Diced green chilies
* Sweetened condensed milk: For dessert recipes
* Peanut butter or other favorite nut butters

Dry Goods for Baking

Many bakers prefer to use all-purpose flour, which requires that you also stock baking powder and baking soda. My grandmother taught me to make biscuits using self-rising flour, so it's what I know and my usual preference. However, I sometimes like incorporating more whole grains and have started using white whole-wheat flour in muffins and pancakes like my Hearty Whole-Grain Pancakes (see page 37), which comes from white wheat berries and still has the whole grain intact for full fiber and a lovely flavor.

* Self-rising flour (or all-purpose if you prefer)
* White whole-wheat flour
* Baking powder and baking soda (when using all-purpose or white whole-wheat flour)
* Sugar or coconut sugar: If you are concerned about refined sugars, coconut sugar is a good one-to-one substitute.
* Brown sugar
* Confectioner's or powdered sugar
* Cornstarch: This works as a good thickening agent. We will learn how to make a slurry by whisking together equal parts water and cornstarch and slowly adding it to simmering soup or stew to thicken the broth.
* Cornmeal: Of course, this Southern girl loves making cornbread, but I also like to use a sprinkle of cornmeal on a greased pan before spreading out pizza dough, which gives the crust a nice texture.
* Chocolate chips
* Dutch unsweetened cocoa powder
* Flaked coconut
* Nuts: Pecans, walnuts, almonds

Grains and Pasta

We eat a lot of pasta at our house, so I stock our pantry with a variety of noodles. Many brands now offer whole-wheat pastas, which are lower in calories and have more indigestible fiber for a healthier meal.

* Long-grain rice: Basmati or jasmine
* Brown rice or wild rice
* Quinoa or farro: I don't usually stock both, but I do like incorporating one of these healthy grains into salads.
* Old-fashioned rolled oats
* Pasta: Lasagna noodles, spaghetti or angel hair noodles, and macaroni
* Breadcrumbs: Panko and Italian

Dry Herbs, Spices, and Extracts

As the famous chef James Beard once said, "Where would we be without salt?" Not appealing on its own, salt enhances the flavor of almost every food and is used in most baking recipes. It's probably the most essential spice you have in your pantry. A well-stocked kitchen has salt as well as these other useful and frequently used spices.

* Salt: Kosher salt and sea salt
* Black pepper: I use a lot of freshly ground pepper, so my pantry is stocked with black peppercorns.
* Ground cinnamon
* Ground ginger
* Nutmeg
* Cumin
* Smoked paprika
* Chili powder
* Red chili flakes and red cayenne pepper
* Onion and garlic powders
* Dried thyme and oregano: For when I don't have fresh
* Flavor extracts: At a minimum, vanilla, but almond, lemon, and peppermint extracts are also good to have on hand.

Oils, Vinegars, Condiments, and Sauces

Another essential ingredient for cooking, extra-virgin olive oil is rich in monounsaturated fats—one of the few fats most people agree is healthy. Olive oil is also useful for sautéing, roasting vegetables, and making vinaigrettes and sauces. Olive oil, other oils, and vinegars that will help complete your pantry include:

* Extra-virgin olive oil: Oils that say "light" will not have as much flavor.
* Sesame oil: Also known for its health benefits, a few drops of sesame oil add a boost of flavor to many Asian-style and stir-fry recipes.
* Canola oil: For frying
* Cooking spray
* Balsamic vinegar: One of my absolute favorite ingredients to add to vinaigrettes, vegetables, and even fruit (see my Balsamic Strawberry Parfaits recipe on page 158)
* Red wine vinegar
* Apple cider vinegar: Either raw or filtered

* Rice wine vinegar: For Asian and stir fry recipes
* Ketchup
* Mustard: Yellow and Dijon
* Mayonnaise: I prefer the olive oil variety, but regular works for all the recipes in this book.
* Soy sauce (low sodium)
* Worcestershire sauce
* Maple syrup
* Honey
* Molasses: I use this ingredient in barbecue sauces and for Christmas baking.
* Hot sauce
* Pickles or relish

Keeping Fresh Herbs Fresh

When you bring fresh herbs home from the grocery store, the first thing you should do is trim the stems and rinse the herbs under cool running water. Dry the herbs thoroughly by laying them out on a paper towel or using a salad spinner. You don't want to leave any extra moisture that might lead to decay. Once the herbs are dry, follow these storage tips:

For parsley, cilantro, dill, tarragon, and mint: Place the herb bunch in a tall glass of cool water and cover loosely with a plastic bag. Store in the refrigerator, changing the water every couple of days.

For basil: Place the herb bunch in a tall glass of water and leave at room temperature on the kitchen counter. If refrigerated, the leaves will turn black.

For rosemary, oregano, thyme, chives, and sage: Wrap the washed and dried herbs loosely in a damp paper towel and place in a sealed container in the refrigerator's crisper drawer.

Weekly Menu Planning Tips

Knowing ahead of time what you're planning to cook for dinner each week is a stress-reducer in itself. Set up a time to draw up a menu (and an accompanying shopping list) for the week. This could be one evening, a weekend morning, or whenever you have a calm moment. The important thing is to be consistent week to week.

Post the menu: Use a chalkboard or dry-erase board to record the week's daily menu. This will help keep it in the front of your mind, even if you hang the menu board on the back of your pantry door.

Plan for leftovers: Double up on recipes so that you cook once and eat twice. Freeze the extra or use leftovers for lunches during the week.

Save and rotate meal plans: Take a photo of your menu board and save it to a smartphone photo album. After you've created a few meal plans, start repeating the ones you like best.

Schedule a night off: Plan for a no-cook meal by including salads or wraps for dinner one evening every week. Look for the No-Cook recipe label; there are several you will love!

Keep a stocked pantry: Cooking and meal planning are easier when the pantry is full.

Sample Weekly Meal Plan

SATURDAY

Breakfast
Sourdough French Toast with Maple Berry Syrup (see page 36)

Lunch
Spinach Salad with Citrus Vinaigrette (see page 42)

Dinner
BBQ Pork Sandwich with Pickled Red Onions (see page 86)
Easy Barbecue Sauce with Molasses (see page 71)

SUNDAY

Breakfast
Egg-in-a-Hash with Sweet Potato and Bacon (see page 34)

Lunch
Roasted Tomato Basil Soup (see page 50)

Dinner
Sunday Roast Chicken (see page 85)
Scalloped Cauliflower (see page 102)

MONDAY

Breakfast
Coconut Granola (see page 26) with fresh fruit and yogurt

Lunch
Greek Grain Chicken Bowls (see page 54) *Use leftovers from Sunday Roast Chicken (see page 85) or a rotisserie chicken and roasted tomatoes*

Dinner
Slow Cooker Beef Pot Roast with Mushrooms (see page 83)
Sour Cream Mashed Potatoes (see page 111)

TUESDAY

Breakfast
Veggie Frittata (see page 32)

Lunch
Cold Roast Beef Sandwiches with Horseradish Aioli (see page 55) *Use leftovers from Slow Cooker Beef Pot Roast with Mushrooms (see page 83)*

Dinner
Sloppy Joes (see page 68)
Tossed salad with Sundried Tomato Vinaigrette (see page 47)

WEDNESDAY

Breakfast
Tropical Smoothie (see page 29)

Lunch
Zesty Chicken Salad (see page 45) *Use leftover Sundried Tomato Vinaigrette (see page 47) and a rotisserie chicken*

Dinner
Shepherd's Pie (see page 87) *Use leftover Sloppy Joes (see page 68) and Sour Cream Mashed Potatoes (see page 111)*

THURSDAY

Breakfast
Coconut Granola (see page 26) with fresh fruit and yogurt

Lunch
Pasta e Fagioli Salad (see page 48)

Dinner
Sheet Pan Sweet and Sour Chicken (see page 66)
Steamed white rice

FRIDAY

Breakfast
Fig Ricotta Toast (see page 30)

Lunch
Pasta e Fagioli Salad (see page 48) *Use leftovers from previous day*

Dinner
Crispy Oven-Fried Fish Sticks (see page 82)
Mexican Zucchini (*Calabacitas*) (see page 99)

* Prep the week's vegetables and salad greens and refrigerate them in resealable plastic bags.
* Bake Coconut Granola (see page 26) for the week.
* Make Roasted Tomato Basil Soup (see page 50) and save some roasted tomatoes for Greek Grain Chicken Bowls (see page 54).
* Make quinoa for Greek Grain Chicken Bowls.

Food Gathering: How to Shop and Get Ahead

Living my own busy life, the last thing I want to do is spend hours shopping for groceries. Adopting the following simple approach will save you valuable time and remove the temptation to purchase unneeded items and junk food.

Make a shopping list: Once you have mapped out your meal plan for the week, it's time to take inventory of what items you'll need. To make shopping trips as efficient as possible, group your shopping list by type since stores are organized by category: produce, dairy, meats, grains, canned goods, and others. You may find that a grocery shopping list smartphone app is helpful for keeping track (for the apps I recommend, see Resources on page 163).

Stock the staples: After taking stock of my cupboard, I do a major shop to restock the staple pantry and freezer items. Staples won't usually need to be replaced again for a few weeks.

Shop the perimeter: On a weekly basis, I shop the perimeter of the grocery store to stock up on the fresh and perishable ingredients I need based on my meal plan. In most grocery stores, fresh produce, the butcher shop or meat counter, deli, and dairy items are along the store's perimeter.

Check out the farmers market: While they may not be available year-round in your region, your local farmers market will have the freshest produce possible. Much of our grocery store produce is picked long before it's ripe so it can be shipped long distances and stored for several days before it's sold. The long storage times and refrigeration change the flavor and, sometimes, the nutritional content of the food. Shopping at farmer's markets is a great way to find freshly picked, in-season food that is bursting with flavor.

Online Grocery Shopping and Delivery

Most major grocery store chains now offer online shopping with convenient pick-up or delivery services. At times, I love the convenience of online grocery shopping, driving to the store, and letting someone else load my groceries in my car—if only they would come home with me and put them away! Online grocery shopping can be a lifesaver when I'm in a crunch. However, I normally prefer to shop for my own meats and produce so I can make sure I'm getting the best quality and freshest items available (for the online grocery shopping options I recommend, see Resources on page 163).

Farm Fresh or Community Farm Produce Subscriptions

The next best thing to visiting the farmers market, some farms offer a fresh produce subscription, sometimes called a share. They are often called CSAs (community-supported agriculture). Farmers pack a box for pickup (or delivery) with produce harvested that week in your area. This is a great opportunity to try vegetables you otherwise might not choose on your own. It also supports local farmers and your local community.

Veggie Frittata, page 32

CHAPTER TWO

Breakfast

Breakfast is often called the most important meal of the day, and I can't say I disagree. Weekday mornings at our house call for easy, healthy breakfasts, but on weekends we're all about big brunches with plenty of bacon. In this chapter, you'll find a few of my favorite on-the-go breakfast recipes, including Turkey Sausage Egg Muffins and my easy Tropical Smoothie—just blend and go. For more relaxed weekends, I like making overnight breakfast casseroles like Crustless Italian Sausage Quiche so I can enjoy sipping my coffee while breakfast bakes itself.

You can take the girl out of the country, but you can't take the country out of the girl.

Growing up, I remember my dad ate a fully-cooked breakfast of fried eggs, sausage or bacon, biscuits and gravy, and homemade blackberry jam or apple butter. Every. Single. Day. He left for work long before the rest of us kids were out of bed, so we usually only had time to eat a quick bowl of oatmeal or cereal before heading off to catch the bus to school. My dad was a physical laborer, so a hearty breakfast was especially important for fueling his day. Bless her heart—for years, my mom got up at 4:30 a.m. to cook his breakfast.

Weekends were different: the whole family ate breakfast together. It was actually my dad who taught me how to make a proper roux for sawmill gravy. Sometimes, Saturday breakfast would include fried country ham my dad had cured himself (we raised a hog each year to slaughter in the fall) and red-eye gravy. If you're not from the South, you might not be familiar with red-eye gravy, a sauce made from country ham pan drippings and strong black coffee. My dad would split open a hot biscuit and ladle on sawmill gravy first, then add a ladleful of the salty red-eye gravy. I usually preferred to add a big slice of tomato to my gravy and biscuit. During the summer months, there was always a plate of ripe tomatoes on the table at every meal. I ate them up!

Back then, no one seemed too concerned about the amount of cholesterol or fat in their diet. Truthfully, it wasn't much of an issue because the people in my circle were all physically active. We now know that, along with reducing saturated fats in your diet, staying active is associated with healthy cholesterol levels. As a rule these days, I try to use low-fat dairy products in my cooking. Every little bit helps, right?

Today, breakfast at our house looks a lot different from my childhood. On weekdays, we opt for something quick—but still wholesome—like Fig Ricotta Toast (see page 30). You can bet my dad would never have gone for that! Often, I'll prep breakfast foods we can reheat and take with us, or I'll make a batch of homemade Coconut Granola (see page 26) we can enjoy the entire week with Greek yogurt and fresh fruit.

We still like to splurge on weekends, but we reserve the country ham for our traditional Christmas brunch. Like my dad, my husband likes to cook on Saturday mornings, and not only does he make a classic English toad-in-the-hole, he also does an amazing job flipping pancakes on the griddle. The Hearty Whole-Grain Pancakes (see page 37) are especially delicious with the fresh berries we get from my father-in-law's blueberry bushes.

Living my "city" life, I don't cook my dad's country breakfast often, but, when I do, it's most certainly a treat. You'll see in the following recipes that I'll always be a country girl at heart.

Baked Blueberry Oatmeal

This recipe has a wonderful aroma! Your family will wake up thinking you've made oatmeal cookies for breakfast. Bursting with fresh blueberries, this warm oatmeal is delicious on its own, but add a dollop of yogurt or a drizzle of honey if you'd like.

Cooking spray

2 cups old-fashioned rolled oats

⅓ cup coconut sugar

1 teaspoon ground cinnamon

1½ teaspoons baking powder

½ teaspoon kosher salt

2 tablespoons coconut oil, melted

2 cups milk

1 egg, beaten

2 teaspoons vanilla extract

1⅓ cups blueberries, divided

ONE-POT
NUT-FREE
SOY-FREE
VEGETARIAN

SERVES: **6**

Per Serving

Calories: 264; Total Fat: 9g;
Saturated Fat: 6g;
Carbohydrates: 41g;
Fiber: 4g; Protein: 8g

1. Preheat the oven to 375°F.

2. Lightly coat a 9-by-9-inch square baking pan with cooking spray. Stir together the oats, coconut sugar, cinnamon, baking powder, and salt in a large bowl.

3. Add the coconut oil, milk, egg, and vanilla extract to the large bowl. Stir until combined. Fold in 1 cup of the blueberries and pour into the prepared baking pan. Sprinkle the remaining blueberries on the top.

4. Bake for 30 to 35 minutes or until the oatmeal is set. Cool for 5 minutes, then spoon into bowls and serve.

Crustless Italian Sausage Quiche

Italian sausage adds distinct spice and flavor to this indulgent egg dish that bakes in a deep-dish pie plate and makes its own golden crust.

½ pound bulk Italian sausage (see Tip)

8 ounces mushrooms, sliced

1½ cups shredded Swiss cheese

6 large eggs

½ cup half-and-half (or low-fat milk)

½ teaspoon ground mustard

½ teaspoon kosher salt

¼ teaspoon freshly ground black pepper

1 teaspoon fresh rosemary, minced

MAKE-AHEAD
NUT-FREE
SOY-FREE
GLUTEN-FREE

SERVES: 6

Per Serving

Calories: 298; Total Fat: 22g;
Saturated Fat: 10g;
Carbohydrates: 4g;
Fiber: 1g; Protein: 21g

Tip:

* Italian bulk sausage is often sold in one-pound packages. Cook the entire package, then freeze or save half for other recipes, like an Italian version of the Turkey Sausage Egg Muffins (see page 27).

1. Crumble the sausage into a large skillet and sauté over medium high heat for 5 to 6 minutes, until cooked through. Drain the sausage on paper towels, then add to a lightly greased deep-dish pie plate.

2. Pour off all but a tablespoon of the grease, then add the mushrooms and cook for 2 to 3 minutes, until browned. Use a slotted spoon to remove mushrooms and layer them on top of sausage, then sprinkle with the shredded Swiss cheese.

3. Whisk together the eggs, half-and-half, mustard, salt, and black pepper. Pour the egg mixture over the cheese. Sprinkle with the fresh rosemary. Cover with plastic wrap and chill overnight.

4. Preheat the oven to 375°F. Uncover and bake for 40 to 45 minutes until set and golden brown. Let stand for 5 to 10 minutes before cutting.

Coconut Granola

I often make a batch of crunchy Coconut Granola over the weekend and enjoy it for breakfast all week.

4 cups old-fashioned rolled oats

1½ cups sweetened flaked coconut

1 cup chopped pecans (or almonds)

1 teaspoon ground cinnamon

⅓ cup coconut oil

½ cup coconut sugar

2 teaspoons vanilla extract

1. Preheat the oven to 275°F.

2. Combine the oats, flaked coconut, pecans, and cinnamon in a large bowl.

3. Melt the coconut oil by leaving it in a bowl in a warm area in your home. Once melted, stir in the coconut sugar and vanilla extract. Pour the mixture over the oats and stir gently until all the dry ingredients are evenly coated. Spread the granola evenly onto a jelly roll pan or a large rimmed cookie sheet.

4. Bake for 45 to 60 minutes, stirring every 15 minutes, until golden brown. Watch carefully during last 15 minutes to prevent overbrowning. Remove from the oven and cool completely before storing in an airtight container. Serve with milk or Greek yogurt and fresh berries.

MAKE-AHEAD
SOY-FREE
VEGAN

YIELDS **6 CUPS**
(12 SERVINGS)

Per Serving

Calories: 278; Total Fat: 16g;
Saturated Fat: 9g;
Carbohydrates: 31g;
Fiber: 5g; Protein: 6g

Use the Leftovers:

★ You will use this recipe for my Balsamic Strawberry Parfaits (see page 158).

Flavor Swaps:

★ If you don't normally stock coconut oil, you may substitute melted vegan butter instead.

★ You may substitute an equal amount of brown sugar for the coconut sugar, but keep in mind that the coconut sugar contributes to the wonderful overall coconut flavor.

Turkey Sausage Egg Muffins

PREP TIME: 15 MINUTES / COOK TIME: 25 MINUTES

Do you sometimes feel that you don't have time for anything other than cold cereal for breakfast? Bake a batch of these savory Turkey Sausage Egg Muffins during a free moment on the weekend to reheat in the microwave for a quick and hot on-the-go breakfast throughout the week.

2 cups frozen diced onions and bell peppers

1¾ cups almond flour

2 teaspoons baking powder

1 teaspoon kosher salt

¾ teaspoon freshly ground black pepper

8 ounces turkey sausage, fully cooked and crumbled

6 eggs, lightly beaten

1⅓ cups low-fat cottage cheese

Paprika or red cayenne pepper

1. Preheat the oven to 375°F. Place paper liners in a 12-cup muffin pan.

2. Place the diced onions and bell peppers in a microwave-safe dish and cover with a damp paper towel. Microwave for 30 to 45 seconds, or until cooked and tender. Let cool.

3. In a large bowl, whisk together the almond flour, baking powder, salt, and black pepper. Add the cooked and crumbled turkey sausage, eggs, and onions and bell peppers. Stir gently. Add the cottage cheese and stir until incorporated.

MAKE-AHEAD
GLUTEN-FREE
SOY-FREE

SERVES: 12

Per Serving

Calories: 151; Total Fat: 9g;
Saturated Fat: 2g;
Carbohydrates: 5g;
Fiber: 1g; Protein: 13g

Substitution Tips:

* For a cheesier flavor, reduce the cottage cheese to ⅔ cup and add ⅔ cup shredded cheddar cheese.
* For convenience, this recipe uses fully cooked and crumbled turkey sausage, but you may also use any ground turkey sausage you cook and crumble.

Continued ▸

4. Spoon the mixture into prepared muffin pan using a ⅓-cup measuring cup. Sprinkle the tops with a dash of paprika.

5. Bake for about 25 minutes, or until a toothpick inserted in the center of a muffin comes out clean. Let cool in pan for about 5 minutes.

6. Serve immediately or store the leftovers in a tightly covered container in refrigerator. Reheat a single muffin in microwave for about 30 seconds.

Tropical Smoothie

One sip of this Tropical Smoothie and you'll be dreaming of sand between your toes and waves crashing on the shore no matter what the weather is outside.

2 bananas, peeled and cut into chunks

2 cups frozen mango

Juice from 2 oranges (or ½ cup orange juice)

1 cup Greek yogurt

2 tablespoons honey

Place all the ingredients into a blender and process until smooth. Serve immediately.

NO-COOK
NUT-FREE
SOY-FREE
VEGETARIAN

SERVES: 2

Per Serving

Calories: 371; Total Fat: 3g; Saturated Fat: 2g; Carbohydrates: 79g; Fiber: 6g; Protein: 13g

Flavor Swaps:

* Use frozen pineapple or frozen blueberries in place of the mango.
* Garnish with a fresh orange slice.

Tip:

* Use frozen fruit in smoothies instead of ice, which can sometimes end up chunky and water down the smoothie's flavor.

Fig Ricotta Toast

PREP TIME: 5 MINUTES

Both sweet and savory, my Fig Ricotta Toast is a delightful breakfast that is made with whipped low-fat ricotta cheese, arugula, and dried black mission figs. It is an amazingly tasty recipe that takes only five minutes to make.

1 cup low-fat ricotta cheese

½ teaspoon lemon juice

½ tablespoon extra-virgin olive oil

Sea salt

4 slices toasted sourdough (or whole-grain bread)

1 cup arugula

½ cup dried (or fresh, if preferred) black mission figs, halved

Honey

Freshly ground black pepper

1. Make the whipped ricotta by whisking the ricotta cheese with the lemon juice, olive oil, and a sprinkle of sea salt.

2. Spread each slice of toasted bread with the whipped ricotta.

3. Pile arugula and sliced figs onto each slice of toast and drizzle with honey. Season with the black pepper. Serve immediately, open-faced.

NO-COOK
NUT-FREE
SOY-FREE
VEGETARIAN

SERVES: **4**

Per Serving

Calories: 220; Total Fat: 8g;
Saturated Fat: 4g;
Carbohydrates: 29g;
Fiber: 4g; Protein: 11g

Flavor Swap:

★ Add a slice or two of Italian salami for a more savory breakfast toast.

Veggie Frittata

PREP TIME: 5 MINUTES / COOK TIME: 25 MINUTES

A frittata is the next best thing to a fancy breakfast quiche, only it comes together with much less effort! This Greek-inspired frittata is flavored with fresh oregano and feta cheese.

1 tablespoon extra-virgin olive oil

1 red bell pepper, diced

⅓ cup red onion, diced

¾ teaspoon kosher salt, divided

2 cups baby spinach

8 large eggs

2 tablespoons warm water

¼ teaspoon freshly ground black pepper

4 ounces feta cheese crumbles

1 teaspoon chopped fresh oregano or basil

EASY CLASSIC
GLUTEN-FREE
SOY-FREE
VEGETARIAN

SERVES: 6

Per Serving

Calories: 175; Total Fat: 13g; Saturated Fat: 5g; Carbohydrates: 4g; Fiber: 1g; Protein: 12g

Flavor Swap:

★ Diced zucchini instead of the spinach is another tasty vegetable option for this recipe.

1. Preheat the oven to 350°F. Heat the olive oil in a large oven-proof skillet (I like to use my cast iron) over medium heat. Add the bell pepper and onion. Sprinkle with ¼ teaspoon salt and add the oregano. Sauté for about 5 minutes, or until the veggies are tender.

2. Add the baby spinach and cook for 2 to 3 minutes, until wilted. Spread the veggies evenly around the pan.

3. Whisk the eggs with the warm water. Add in the rest of the salt, black pepper, and feta cheese. Then the pour the egg mixture over the veggies in the skillet.

4. Cook for about 5 minutes, or until the eggs begin to set along the pan's edge. Run a spatula around edge to allow the uncooked eggs to run underneath. Cook for a couple more minutes and repeat this procedure.

5. Remove from heat and place the frittata in the preheated oven. Bake for about 15 minutes, or until the eggs are set. Place the frittata under the broiler for a couple of minutes to brown top. Cut into wedges and serve.

Egg-in-a-Hash with Sweet Potato and Bacon

PREP TIME: 10 MINUTES / COOK TIME: 20 MINUTES

Breakfast hash made with sweet potatoes (in place of white potatoes) will save you a few carbs and calories. Their natural sweetness is delicious paired with bacon and fresh rosemary in this hearty breakfast recipe.

4 slices bacon

2 large sweet potatoes, peeled and diced

½ cup onion, diced

2 teaspoons fresh rosemary, minced

1 teaspoon salt, plus more for seasoning if desired

½ teaspoon freshly ground black pepper, plus more for seasoning if desired

4 eggs

1. Preheat the oven to 400°F.

2. Cook the bacon in a large cast-iron skillet (or another oven-proof pan) over medium-low heat for 6 to 7 minutes, depending on thickness of slices, until crisp. Remove to a paper-towel lined plate to drain. Drain the bacon fat from pan, reserving 2 tablespoons.

3. Add the diced sweet potatoes and onion to the pan with the reserved fat. Cover and cook for 5 to 6 minutes over medium heat, stirring occasionally.

EASY CLASSIC
DAIRY-FREE
GLUTEN-FREE
SOY-FREE

SERVES: 4

Per Serving

Calories: 230; Total Fat: 13g; Saturated Fat: 4g; Carbohydrates: 16g; Fiber: 3g; Protein: 14g

Flavor Swaps:

* To make vegetarian, leave out bacon; cook the onion and sweet potatoes in 2 tablespoons of olive oil.

Tip:

* When cooking sweet potatoes in cast iron, the natural sugars tend to burn quickly. Watch carefully and adjust the heat to avoid burning.

4. Turn off the burner. Crumble the bacon and add it to the pan along with the rosemary, salt, and black pepper. Stir to combine. Make 4 wells in the mixture and crack an egg into each one. Sprinkle the eggs with a little salt and black pepper (if desired).

5. Place the pan in the oven and bake for 6 to 10 minutes, depending on if you prefer eggs sunny-side up or cooked through. Serve immediately.

Sourdough French Toast with Maple Berry Syrup

PREP TIME: 5 MINUTES / COOK TIME: 8 TO 10 MINUTES

This French toast is wonderful and has a classic flavor. The best part: You can customize it by using your favorite pure fruit spread to make the Maple Berry Syrup.

2 eggs

½ cup milk

½ teaspoon vanilla extract

¼ cup plus 2 tablespoons maple syrup, divided

8 (¾-inch) slices sourdough bread

¾ cup pure fruit spread (strawberry, blackberry, or raspberry)

Cooking spray (or melted butter)

1. Whisk together the eggs, milk, vanilla extract, and 2 tablespoons maple syrup in a shallow baking dish. Dip the sourdough bread slices in the mixture, turning to coat all sides.

2. Heat the pure fruit spread with the remaining ¼ cup maple syrup in a small saucepan over medium heat until melted. Reduce heat to low to keep syrup warm until ready to serve.

3. Heat a large nonstick griddle or skillet over medium heat. Spray lightly with cooking spray (or brush with melted butter) and add the soaked bread—work in batches if needed. Cook for about 4 minutes on each side, or until browned.

4. Serve immediately with the syrup on the side.

EASY CLASSIC SOY-FREE VEGETARIAN

SERVES: **4**

Per Serving

Calories: 436; Total Fat: 4g; Saturated Fat: 1g; Carbohydrates: 88g; Fiber: 2g; Protein: 12g

Tip:

* Serve with additional fresh berries; you could even use matching berries to the fruit spread for the ultimate berry flavor.

Hearty Whole-Grain Pancakes

PREP TIME: 5 MINUTES / COOK TIME: 10 MINUTES

The flour in these pancakes still has the whole grain intact for full fiber and a lovely flavor. Serve with warmed maple syrup and fresh berries for a wholesome breakfast.

1½ cups whole-wheat white flour

3 tablespoons coconut sugar

⅓ cup old-fashioned rolled oats

1 egg, beaten

1¼ cups low-fat milk

3 tablespoons butter, melted and cooled slightly

1. Preheat a nonstick griddle to 350°F or preheat a large skillet over medium heat.

2. Combine the whole-wheat white flour, coconut sugar, and oats in a large bowl. Whisk together the egg, milk, and melted butter in another bowl until combined.

3. Add the wet ingredients to the dry ingredients and stir with a fork until combined with a few lumps remaining—the batter should be thick.

4. Spoon the batter onto the griddle and cook for about 3 minutes, until bubbles form on the surface. Flip and cook on other side for about 3 minutes, until browned.

EASY CLASSIC
NUT-FREE
SOY-FREE
VEGETARIAN

SERVES: 5

Per Serving

Calories: 296; Total Fat: 10g;
Saturated Fat: 5g;
Carbohydrates: 45g;
Fiber: 5g; Protein: 10g

Flavor Swaps:

★ Serve warm with maple syrup and fresh berries, if you desire.

★ Granulated sugar may be substituted for the coconut sugar.

★ Add a few toasted pecans or walnuts to the pancake batter if you'd like a bit of crunch.

Quick Korean Lettuce
Wraps, page 53

CHAPTER THREE

Lunch

When it comes to lunch, what's your normal go-to grub—soup, salad, sandwich? If you're like me, when life gets busy, it's easy to get in a rut and eat the same boring thing for lunch day after day. In this chapter, I'll help you mix things up with both new and classic recipes for a creative assortment of fresh lunch options, such as Quick Korean Lettuce Wraps or my take on Pasta e Fagioli, in salad form. Here, you'll find hearty and warming soups, gourmet sandwich combinations, make-ahead salads, and plenty of vegetarian options as well.

How I finally learned to meal prep a week's worth of lunches.

I'd like to say I taught my daughters to prep and plan meals to make their professional lives easier, but that's not exactly the case. In fact, it was my youngest daughter who inspired me to start seriously prepping and planning meals that included well-balanced lunches for the week ahead. I had slipped into the habit of eating lunch out every day—mostly because I'm not a morning person and could never manage packing my lunch before it was time to leave.

As a single young professional with a very busy work schedule, my daughter is the queen of Sunday night meal prep. She finds recipes she wants to try, makes a list, grocery shops Sunday afternoons, then comes home to cook for the week—even stocking her freezer with make-ahead dishes. She invested in multiple sets of single-serving resealable containers for portioning out soups, salads, and wraps. A week's worth of easy grab-and-go lunches, dinners, and snacks sit on her refrigerator shelves labeled and sorted, showing off her supply-chain management skills at home.

Getting into the habit of meal prepping, even if it's only lunches for the week, really pays off—I mean that literally. By packing a lunch, you will automatically save money. Eating out can get expensive, even when it's fast food. A packaged salad or burger and fries can easily cost $8 to $10 or more every day. For what you'd spend in a week, you could be eating more nutritious, wholesome lunches, like my fresh Spinach Salad with Citrus Vinaigrette (see page 42) or filling Greek Grain Chicken Bowl (see page 54).

For me, prepping lunches helped me cut down on the amount of salty, processed foods in my diet. I'm sad to say I have quite the taste for salt and vinegar potato chips and ordered a bag to go along with a big sub sandwich from the deli at least three or four days a week. Oh, I still enjoy eating those salty, crunchy chips, but now I only eat them occasionally instead of daily. Also, when I started meal prepping lunches and snacks for work, I became more intentional about portion control—another added benefit!

Trying to pack a lunch in the morning was too stressful for me, even if it was leftovers from the previous night's dinner. But, doing it all ahead of time was different—no more mornings spent staring into the refrigerator last-minute, wondering if there was anything to take for lunch. Once the meal plan was executed, I could just grab-and-go, knowing that my lunch would be fresher and healthier, too.

If you're already in the habit of meal prepping lunches for the week, good for you! If you're late to the party like me, I hope the recipes in this chapter will inspire you.

Spinach Salad with Citrus Vinaigrette

PREP TIME: 15 MINUTES

This salad has bright and fresh flavors because of the balance between the sweetness of the fruit and the tanginess of the dressing.

3 navel oranges, divided

½ shallot, minced

1½ tablespoons white wine vinegar

½ teaspoon dried oregano

¾ cup extra-virgin olive oil

6 cups baby spinach

1 cup sliced strawberries

½ cup blue cheese crumbles

1. To make the vinaigrette: Juice and zest one of the oranges in a small bowl. Add the shallot, white wine vinegar, and oregano and stir to combine. Slowly pour in the olive oil and whisk until dressing is emulsified.

2. Peel the remaining oranges, removing as much pith as possible and separating both oranges into segments.

3. Place the orange segments, spinach, and strawberries in a large salad bowl. Add the vinaigrette a little at a time and toss to coat the salad (you should have leftover vinaigrette to use another time). Top with blue cheese crumbles and serve.

NO-COOK
NUT-FREE
GLUTEN-FREE
SOY-FREE
VEGETARIAN

SERVES: 4

Per Serving

Calories: 463; Total Fat: 42g;
Saturated Fat: 8g;
Carbohydrates: 22g;
Fiber: 5g; Protein: 5g

Tips:

★ If available, add a tablespoon of chopped fresh oregano to the vinaigrette for extra freshness.

★ Instead of whisking the vinaigrette, add the ingredients to a sealed Mason jar and shake to combine.

★ Store leftover vinaigrette in the refrigerator for up to a week.

Caesar-Style Kale Salad

PREP TIME: 20 MINUTES

Let's reimagine Caesar Salad by substituting kale—one of the top-rated super foods—for the traditional romaine lettuce. Kale is a low-calorie, high fiber food with many health benefits, and it's a good source of iron, too.

6 tablespoons low-fat mayonnaise

3 tablespoons red wine vinegar

2 garlic cloves, minced

¼ cup freshly grated Parmesan cheese, divided

Sea salt

Freshly ground black pepper

1 bunch kale, leaves removed from stems

1. In a small bowl, whisk together the mayonnaise, red wine vinegar, garlic, and 2 tablespoons of Parmesan cheese. Season to taste with sea salt and black pepper.

2. Roughly chop the kale leaves and place them in a large bowl. Pour the dressing over the kale and toss to coat. Using your hands, gently massage kale for a couple of minutes to soften. Refrigerate until ready to serve.

3. To serve, sprinkle the salad with the remaining 2 tablespoons of Parmesan cheese.

NO-COOK
EASY CLASSIC
NUT-FREE
GLUTEN-FREE
VEGETARIAN

SERVES: 4

Per Serving

Calories: 114; Total Fat: 5g;
Saturated Fat: 1g;
Carbohydrates: 14g;
Fiber: 2g; Protein: 5g

Tips:

* Kale is more difficult to chew than the romaine lettuce in a traditional Caesar salad. Because of this, be sure to chop the kale leaves into smaller pieces than you would lettuce. Also, don't skip massaging the dressing into the kale—this will make it softer and easier to chew.

Santa Fe Rice Salad

PREP TIME: 15 MINUTES / COOK TIME: 15 MINUTES

Make the rice and grilled corn for this zesty Tex-Mex salad ahead of time and chill them in the refrigerator. Then, toss with the remaining ingredients and a bright cilantro-lime dressing for a salad that can double as a workday lunch or a side dish for taco night.

For the salad:

2 ears corn

Extra-virgin olive oil

Kosher salt

Freshly ground black pepper

2 cups cooked white rice, chilled in the refrigerator

1 (15-ounce) can black beans, rinsed and drained

1 cup cherry tomatoes, diced

For the vinaigrette:

Juice from 1 lime

¼ cup extra-virgin olive oil

¼ cup cilantro leaves, chopped

1 garlic clove, minced

1 teaspoon kosher salt

¼ teaspoon coriander

1 teaspoon honey

1. Brush the corn with olive oil and season with salt and black pepper. Grill over high heat for 5 to 6 minutes, rotating often until the corn has charred spots. Cool and cut kernels off the cob.

2. Mix the corn, rice, beans, and tomatoes in a bowl.

3. To make the vinaigrette: Whisk together the lime juice, olive oil, cilantro, garlic, salt, coriander, and honey. Save the vinaigrette on the side. Then, pour it over corn and rice mixture. Stir and serve.

MAKE-AHEAD
DAIRY-FREE
SOY-FREE
VEGETARIAN

SERVES: **6**

Per Serving

Calories: 211; Total Fat: 9g; Saturated Fat: 1g; Carbohydrates: 30g; Fiber: 3g; Protein: 4g

Use the Leftovers:

★ While the grill is hot, throw on extra corn cobs to make my Street Corn Salad (see page 104).

Flavor Swaps:

★ Substitute pinto beans for the black beans.
★ Try adding diced red bell pepper or avocado to the salad.

Zesty Chicken Salad

PREP TIME: 15 MINUTES

Everyone at my house devoured this Zesty Chicken Salad in minutes the first time I made it! Using leftover Sundried Tomato Vinaigrette and a rotisserie chicken makes preparing this recipe super easy. Don't skip the fresh basil—it definitely amps up the flavor.

1 rotisserie chicken, shredded (about 3 cups of meat)

½ cup low-fat mayonnaise

6 tablespoons Sundried Tomato Vinaigrette (see page 47)

½ teaspoon salt

2 tablespoons minced fresh basil

Freshly ground black pepper

1. Place the shredded chicken in a large bowl.

2. In a smaller bowl, whisk together the mayonnaise, Sundried Tomato Vinaigrette, and salt. Add the mixture to the chicken along with the minced basil. Stir gently to combine. Garnish with freshly ground black pepper.

NO-COOK
REINVENTION
NUT-FREE
DAIRY-FREE

SERVES: 6

Per Serving

Calories: 287; Total Fat: 20g; Saturated Fat: 3g; Carbohydrates: 5g; Fiber: 0g; Protein: 20g

Tip:

★ Make chicken stock from the leftover chicken carcass. Add the chicken skin and bones to a large stock pot with onion, celery, and thyme. Cover with water and simmer for about an hour. Strain the stock, cool completely, then seal tightly and freeze for later use.

Banana "Party" Pepper Tuna Salad

PREP TIME: 15 MINUTES

My daughter and her friends love topping pepperoni pizza with banana peppers. After one of her crew brought a gallon of pickled banana pepper rings to a pizza party—and left them afterwards—the "party peppers" started traveling from house to house. "I'll bring the party peppers!" has become a running joke and the inspiration for this recipe. Party peppers definitely give classic tuna salad some zing.

2 (10-ounce) cans white albacore tuna, drained

1 stalk celery, finely diced

2 green onions, finely diced

⅓ cup mild banana pepper rings, chopped, and
   2 tablespoons of the pickle juice

⅓ cup low-fat mayonnaise

½ teaspoon dried dill

¼ teaspoon kosher salt

⅛ teaspoon freshly ground black pepper

1. Place the tuna in a medium-size bowl. Flake it with a fork to break up the chunks. Add the celery, green onions, and banana peppers and stir to combine.

2. In a small bowl, whisk together 2 tablespoons of the banana pepper pickle juice, the mayonnaise, dried dill, salt, and black pepper. Add the mixture to the tuna and stir until all ingredients are coated. Refrigerate until chilled for the best flavor.

NO-COOK
EASY CLASSIC
NUT-FREE
DAIRY-FREE

SERVES: **4**

Per Serving

Calories: 104; Total Fat: 4g;
Saturated Fat: 0g;
Carbohydrates: 4g;
Fiber: 0g; Protein: 14g

Tips:
* If available, use fresh dill for heightened flavor.
* Try serving this dish in a tomato cup. Cut the tomatoes into six wedges, but not all the way through. Separate the wedges slightly and place a scoop of tuna salad in the center.

Sundried Tomato Vinaigrette

PREP TIME: 10 MINUTES

This simple vinaigrette is tremendously versatile. Drizzle it on a tossed green salad, use it to marinate mozzarella cheese as an appetizer spread, dress a pasta salad, or use it to make my Zesty Chicken Salad (see page 45). This is what this book is all about—using a delicious recipe it in a number of different ways.

4 sundried tomato halves packed in oil, plus 2 tablespoons of the oil

6 tablespoons extra-virgin olive oil

3 tablespoons apple cider vinegar

1 tablespoon balsamic vinegar (or balsamic reduction)

1 teaspoon fresh oregano leaves

½ teaspoon kosher salt

¼ teaspoon freshly ground black pepper

1. Place the sundried tomato halves in a food processor or blender and pulse for a few seconds to finely chop.

2. Add the remaining ingredients and process until the vinaigrette is emulsified. Use immediately or store in the refrigerator for up to a week.

MAKE-AHEAD
NO-COOK
NUT-FREE
GLUTEN-FREE
VEGAN

YIELDS ¾ CUP

Per Serving (2 tablespoons)

Calories: 189; Total Fat: 19g; Saturated Fat: 3g; Carbohydrates: 4g; Fiber: 1g; Protein: 1g

Tip:

* The oil in this vinaigrette may congeal after being refrigerated. To serve, allow to sit at room temperature for about 30 minutes until the oil has liquified. You may also microwave on 50 percent power for about 30 seconds, then give it a quick stir or whisk before using it.

Pasta e Fagioli Salad

PREP TIME: 15 MINUTES / COOK TIME: 15 MINUTES

In this recipe, we will transform an all-time favorite Italian soup into a fresh and delicious pasta salad dressed with a delightful lemon dressing.

2 quarts water

8 ounces small ditalini pasta (or small farfalle/
  bowtie pasta)

1 (15-ounce) can cannellini beans, rinsed
  and drained

2 Roma tomatoes, diced

2 scallions (or green onions), diced

1 tablespoon fresh lemon juice

1 teaspoon lemon zest

3 tablespoons extra-virgin olive oil

2 tablespoons minced fresh flat-leaf Italian parsley

Kosher salt

Freshly ground black pepper

EASY CLASSIC
NUT-FREE
DAIRY-FREE
VEGAN

SERVES: **4**

Per Serving

Calories: 391; Total Fat: 12g;
Saturated Fat: 2g;
Carbohydrates: 59g;
Fiber: 8g; Protein: 12g

1. Bring 2 quarts of water to a boil in a large stock pot. Add the pasta and cook for about 7 to 8 minutes, until al dente. Drain and rinse with cold running water.

2. Place the pasta in a large bowl. Add the beans, tomatoes, and scallions. Toss gently.

3. Add the lemon juice and zest, olive oil, and parsley, and toss gently until combined. Season with salt and black pepper to taste. Serve immediately or refrigerate and serve chilled.

Gazpacho

PREP TIME: 15 MINUTES / CHILL TIME: 2 HOURS

This soup is like summertime in a bowl! All the best garden vegetables are puréed into this cold and absolutely refreshing soup. Serve it with toasted croutons or a drizzle of aged balsamic vinegar.

2 pounds ripe red tomatoes

½ English cucumber, peeled

½ green bell pepper, cored and seeded

½ small sweet onion, peeled

1 garlic clove, peeled

¼ cup fresh basil leaves

2 tablespoons red wine vinegar

2½ tablespoons extra-virgin olive oil

1 teaspoon kosher salt

½ teaspoon freshly ground black pepper

½ teaspoon cumin

1. Core the tomatoes and cut them into large chunks (no need to peel). Place the tomatoes into the bowl of a blender or food processor.

2. Cut the cucumber, bell pepper, and onion into large chunks and add to blender bowl along with garlic and basil.

3. Add the red wine vinegar, olive oil, salt, black pepper, and cumin. Process or blend for about 2 minutes, until smooth. Cover and chill for two hours to allow flavors to meld.

ONE-POT
NO-COOK
EASY CLASSIC
NUT-FREE
GLUTEN-FREE
VEGAN

SERVES: **4**

Per Serving

Calories: 134; Total Fat: 9g; Saturated Fat: 1g; Carbohydrates: 13g; Fiber: 3g; Protein: 3g

Serving Ideas:

* You can garnish chilled gazpacho with croutons and a drizzle of olive oil or balsamic vinegar. It's also nice to garnish with extra diced veggies like tomatoes, cucumber, or green bell pepper.

Roasted Tomato Basil Soup

Roasting grape tomatoes brings out their natural sweetness in this classic tomato soup recipe. For even more basil freshness, sprinkle a little extra on top of each serving.

2 pints grape tomatoes

1 small onion, cut into slices or thin wedges

4 garlic cloves, peeled

2 tablespoons extra-virgin olive oil

½ teaspoon kosher salt, plus more to taste

½ teaspoon freshly ground black pepper, plus more to taste

1 (32-ounce) carton vegetable broth

¼ cup cornstarch (or all-purpose flour)

½ cup half-and-half (or low-fat milk)

2 tablespoons minced fresh basil leaves

1. Preheat the oven to 400°F. Place the tomatoes, onion, and garlic on a nonstick baking sheet. Drizzle with olive oil, salt, and black pepper. Roast in the oven for 25 minutes.

2. Heat the vegetable broth in a large stock pot over medium-high heat. Once the vegetables are roasted, add them to the broth and purée with an immersion blender (or place them in a food processor and purée before adding it to the broth). Bring the soup to a boil, then reduce heat to low and simmer.

3. Stir cornstarch into the half and half until dissolved. Then, slowly add this mixture to the pot of simmering soup and stir for about 5 minutes, until combined and slightly thickened. Add the basil, then season with salt and black pepper to taste.

**EASY CLASSIC
NUT-FREE
VEGETARIAN**

SERVES: 4

Per Serving

Calories: 190; Total Fat: 11g;
Saturated Fat: 3g;
Carbohydrates: 21g;
Fiber: 4g; Protein: 3g

Tips:

★ Fresh basil loses its delicate flavor and aroma the longer it simmers, which is why we add it at the end of cooking.

★ When eating a bowl of leftover soup, garnish with fresh basil to revive the basil flavor.

Use the Leftovers:

★ Make a double batch of the roasted tomatoes or save a few for my Greek Grain Chicken Bowls (see page 54).

Wild Rice Mushroom Chicken Soup

They say chicken soup is good for the soul, but this one is definitely good for the tummy as well!

1 cup uncooked wild rice, rinsed and drained

1½ pounds boneless, skinless chicken breast

6 cups chicken stock

2 cups white mushrooms, roughly chopped

2 cups Sofritto (see the sidebar on page 61)

2 bay leaves

1½ teaspoons poultry seasoning

1 teaspoon kosher salt

½ teaspoon black pepper

1. Place all the ingredients (including the wild rice) in the slow cooker, making sure the chicken is submerged in the liquid.

2. Cook on low for 6 to 7 hours. Remove the chicken from the soup and use two forks to shred the chicken. Return the shredded chicken to slow cooker and stir it into the soup. Enjoy immediately, or cool completely and refrigerate or freeze for later.

ONE-POT
NUT-FREE
DAIRY-FREE

SERVES: 8

Per Serving

Calories: 192; Total Fat: 3g;
Saturated Fat: 0g;
Carbohydrates: 19g;
Fiber: 2g; Protein: 22g

Tips:

* In leftover soup with rice, the grain tends to absorb the liquid as it sit in the refrigerator. To reheat soups that seem too thick, add a little water or stock to thin it out first.

* To freeze soups, cool completely first. Store in freezer-safe resealable bags in the freezer for up to a month. Thaw for 24 hours in the refrigerator before heating.

Black Bean Sweet Potato Chili

PREP TIME: 10 MINUTES / COOK TIME: 30 MINUTES

Not your typical bowl of chili, this hearty and healthy dish is loaded with big chunks of sweet potatoes, black beans, and savory Italian sausage. It's especially delicious when served with a crusty bread loaf.

1 pound ground Italian sausage (mild or spicy)

1 large sweet potato, peeled and cut into 1-inch chunks

1 large sweet onion, diced

1 garlic clove, minced

2 tablespoons chili powder

2 teaspoons cumin

3 cups water

2 (15-ounce) cans black beans, rinsed and drained

1 (14-ounce) can petite diced tomatoes

ONE-POT
NUT-FREE
DAIRY-FREE
SOY-FREE

SERVES: 6

Per Serving

Calories: 338; Total Fat: 19g; Saturated Fat: 6g; Carbohydrates: 22g; Fiber: 6g; Protein: 19g

Flavor Swap:

* Leave out the ground Italian sausage to make this a vegetarian meal. It is still a hearty chili with the sweet potato and black beans.

1. Crumble the ground Italian sausage into the bottom of a Dutch oven and sauté over medium-high heat for 8 to 10 minutes, until no longer pink.

2. Add the sweet potatoes and onions and cook for about 5 minutes, stirring occasionally. Add the garlic, chili powder, and cumin, stirring constantly for about a minute, until fragrant.

3. Pour in the water and bring it to a boil. Reduce the heat and simmer for about 10 minutes, or until the potatoes are tender.

4. Add the black beans and tomatoes and simmer for another 5 minutes, or until heated through.

Quick Korean Lettuce Wraps

Super tasty and super easy, my Quick Korean Lettuce Wraps can be made with either ground chicken or pork. You can reheat the filling in the microwave, making this a fun lunch to pack for work. It can be served as a party appetizer, too!

4 green onions

1 tablespoon canola oil

1 pound ground chicken or pork

1 garlic clove, minced

1 teaspoon kosher salt

¼ cup low-sodium soy sauce

3 tablespoons sweet chili sauce

Whole romaine or iceberg lettuce leaves

1. Dice the green onions, both white heads and green stems. Save ¼ cup for garnishing.

2. Heat the canola oil in a large skillet over medium-high heat for about 3 minutes. Add the ground chicken or pork to pan and crumble with a wooden spoon. Cook for 5 to 10 minutes, until no pink remains.

3. Drain any grease from the pan. Add the garlic and salt, and cook for about 30 seconds, until garlic is fragrant.

4. Stir in the green onions, soy sauce, and sweet chili sauce and cook a couple of minutes.

5. To serve, spoon about ¼ cup of the meat mixture in the middle of a lettuce leaf and garnish with the remaining green onions.

ONE-POT
NUT-FREE
DAIRY-FREE

SERVES. 4

Per Serving

Calories: 230; Total Fat. 13g;
Saturated Fat: 3g;
Carbohydrates: 9g;
Fiber: 1g; Protein: 21g

Tip:

★ Reheat leftover filling in the microwave covered with a damp paper towel for 30 to 45 seconds.

Greek Grain Chicken Bowls

PREP TIME: 15 MINUTES

Toss a bunch of delicious ingredients into a bowl of high fiber and protein-enriched quinoa for a meal that's nutritious, filling, and wholesome. These Greek Grain Chicken Bowls are perfect for meal prep lunches.

2 cups cooked quinoa

2 cups chopped or shredded deli rotisserie chicken

2 cups roasted grape tomatoes (see step 1 of Roasted Tomato Basil Soup, page 50)

2 cups zucchini, diced

¼ cup pitted kalamata olives, halved

2 tablespoons chopped flat leaf Italian parsley

2 teaspoons chopped mint leaves

2 teaspoons fresh lemon juice

1 tablespoon extra-virgin olive oil

½ teaspoon kosher salt

Freshly ground black pepper

MAKE-AHEAD REINVENTION
NUT-FREE
DAIRY-FREE

SERVES: 4

Per Serving

Calories: 299; Total Fat: 10g; Saturated Fat: 2g; Carbohydrates: 26g; Fiber: 5g; Protein: 27g

Flavor Swap:

★ Add a dollop of Tzatziki Dip (see page 127).

1. Cook the quinoa according to package directions. Divide the quinoa evenly among 4 salad bowls. Top each bowl with ½ cup shredded rotisserie chicken.

2. Mix together the roasted grape tomatoes, zucchini, and kalamata olives in a bowl. Add the Italian parsley, mint, lemon juice, olive oil, and salt. Toss gently.

3. Top the chicken with the salad and garnish with freshly ground black pepper.

Cold Roast Beef Sandwiches with Horseradish Aioli

PREP TIME: 15 MINUTES

This hearty and savory sandwich rivals any gourmet deli creation you've ever tasted. The aioli adds just the right punch to an already mouthwatering combination of tender, flavorful beef roast and nutty arugula.

2 tablespoons prepared horseradish

1 tablespoon Dijon mustard

2 tablespoons low-fat mayonnaise

¼ teaspoon kosher salt

⅛ teaspoon freshly ground black pepper

4 onion rolls, split

3 cups Slow Cooker Beef Pot Roast with Mushrooms (see page 83), shredded

2 cups arugula

1. To make the aioli: In a small bowl, combine the horseradish, Dijon mustard, and mayonnaise. Add salt and black pepper to taste.

2. To make the sandwiches: Spread the aioli on the onion rolls, then pile high with shredded beef and arugula.

REINVENTION
NUT-FREE
DAIRY-FREE

SERVES: 4

Per Serving

Calories: 331; Total Fat: 12g; Saturated Fat: 3g; Carbohydrates: 34g; Fiber: 3g; Protein: 25g

Flavor Swap:

* Add thin slices of red onion or tomato for even more flavor.

Italian Grilled Cheese Panini

PREP TIME: 5 MINUTES / REST TIME: 10 MINUTES / COOK TIME: 18 MINUTES

Prepare the roasted red bell peppers and roasted garlic mayo ahead of time, and refrigerate them until you're ready to make these Mediterranean-inspired grilled cheese paninis.

2 red bell peppers

6 to 7 garlic cloves

Extra-virgin olive oil

¼ cup low-fat mayonnaise

1 loaf sourdough bread, cut into 12 slices

6 slices mozzarella cheese

1 small jar artichoke hearts, drained

Kosher salt

Freshly ground black pepper

MAKE-AHEAD
NUT-FREE
VEGETARIAN

SERVES: **4**

Per Serving
Calories: 427; Total Fat: 13g;
Saturated Fat: 5g;
Carbohydrates: 55g;
Fiber: 4g; Protein: 21g

Tips:
* You can also roast peppers directly over a gas stove burner—just be *very* careful with the open flame.
* Garlic may also be roasted in a 325°F oven for about 30 minutes, or until soft.

1. To roast the bell peppers and garlic: Preheat a grill to high heat. Brush the whole (uncut) bell peppers with olive oil. Grill the peppers with the lid closed for 10 to 12 minutes, turning often, until charred on all sides. At the same time, place the garlic cloves on a double layer of aluminum foil; drizzle with the olive oil and add a pinch of salt, then mix to coat thoroughly. Twist the aluminum foil closed tightly and grill until soft.

2. Once charred, place the peppers in a bowl and cover them tightly with plastic wrap. After about 10 minutes, uncover them and gently remove the skins and seeds. Cut into strips; cover and refrigerate until ready to use.

3. In a bowl, mash the garlic with a fork and stir in the mayonnaise along with a teaspoon of leftover oil from roasting. Refrigerate until ready to use.

4. Build sandwiches by spreading roasted garlic mayo on one side of 4 slices of sourdough.

5. Layer in order: a slice of mozzarella cheese, 1 or 2 artichoke hearts, and a few slices of roasted red peppers. Season with kosher salt and freshly ground pepper. Top with a slice of bread.

6. Heat a grill pan over medium-high heat. Brush one side of the sandwich with olive oil, place it olive oil-side down on hot grill pan, then brush the top side with olive oil. Cook on each side for about 3 minutes, pressing the sandwich down with a wide spatula.

Sunday Roast Chicken, page 85

CHAPTER FOUR

Dinner

"What's for dinner?" is a pretty common question around our house, and I bet it is at yours as well. In this chapter, you'll find some of my favorite easy weeknight recipes, including versions of classic dishes like Sweet and Sour Chicken, Shepherd's Pie, and Sloppy Joes. If you're planning a dinner party with friends, take a look at my restaurant-quality Pan-Seared New York Strip or Rosemary Dijon Chicken Skillet. And don't worry—there are no-cook options, including personal-size Arugula Salad Pizzas. After all, every cook deserves a night off!

I was doing my own cooking therapy before I knew it was a thing.

A few years ago, I realized that even after a particularly hectic day at the office, heading into my kitchen to prepare dinner was actually *therapeutic* for me. The kitchen became my safe haven and a creative outlet that yielded more benefits than just feeding myself. My mind would unwind while my hands worked, chopping vegetables and stirring up sauce. My senses were gratified with the marvelous aroma of fresh herbs, whisking away the day's frenzy. There was a pleasant reward at the end of cooking in a delicious, wholesome meal and the opportunity to connect with my family at the dinner table.

Researchers have found that cooking can help "soothe stress, build self-esteem, and curb negative thinking by focusing the mind on following a recipe."[1] There are even licensed culinary art therapists—yes, cooking therapy is a real thing! According to one expert, "There's a tremendous amount of confidence-boosting and self-esteem boosting, performing an act like cooking for others."[2] Of course, anyone relishes being complimented for a meal they prepared and served to their family or friends. I can attest to that.

But let's get real: Walking into a cluttered, unorganized kitchen, facing a sink full of dirty dishes, and scrambling to find ingredients is hardly the setting for therapeutic or stress-free cooking. Creating a calmer kitchen environment starts with an organized kitchen with a fully-stocked pantry. That kitchen is one that's primed and ready for culinary art therapy at home.

Another kitchen organization principle, *mise en place* (literally "put in place"), can also help set the stage for more efficient, less stressful cooking. This French practice of gathering and arranging ingredients and tools needed to prepare a recipe is taught in most culinary schools, but it's also a good way for home chefs to mindfully approach their kitchens. Think about it—have you ever started a recipe

---

[1] Jeanne Whalen, "A Road to Mental Health Through the Kitchen," *The Wall Street Journal*, December 8, 2014.

[2] Linda Wasmer Andrews, "How Cooking Dinner Helps You Bounce Back from a Tough Day," *Psychology Today*, May 04, 2017.

and found yourself scurrying last-minute to chop or measure the next ingredient to add at the proper time? Practice *mise en place*, and that stressful moment is gone.

Before you start prepping ingredients, always read the recipe through twice: once to review the ingredients and make sure you have everything you need, and again to soak in the instructions so you know the game plan.

Think about cooking dinner at home as your time to unwind. With an organized kitchen, a stocked pantry, and a few simple cooking principles, you'll be set to slow down and breathe. Let your senses soak in the delectable aromas, tastes, and sizzles that you create in your own calm and happy kitchen.

Sofritto: A Chef's Secret

Professional chefs know delicious soups and stews always start with a good chicken, beef, or vegetable stock. They also know that adding *sofritto*—the Italian word for a slow-cooked mixture of diced onions, carrots, and celery, braised in olive oil until soft and caramelized—provides a very pleasing depth of flavor to recipes like my Wild Rice Mushroom Chicken Soup (see page 51). Make a batch of sofritto, and you will have a great aromatic base that can be stored in the refrigerator for up to a week or in a freezer for up to six months. Here's how:

1. Dice onions, carrots, and celery into small, uniform pieces. The ratio for sofritto is always 2:1:1, with onions having the largest amount (for example, 2 cups onion and 1 cup each of carrot and celery).
2. Heat the olive oil over medium heat, then add the diced veggies, and slowly cook for up to 30 minutes, until they turn a golden color.
3. Cool and drain off any extra oil. Store in the refrigerator or freeze.

Rosemary Dijon Chicken Skillet

PREP TIME: 10 MINUTES / COOK TIME: 20 MINUTES

This is a wonderful recipe with tender chicken cutlets that simmer with green beans in a creamy Dijon wine sauce.

⅓ cup all-purpose flour

2½ teaspoons fresh minced rosemary, divided

1 pound chicken cutlets

Kosher salt

Freshly ground black pepper

2 tablespoons extra-virgin olive oil

2 garlic cloves, minced

1½ cups dry white wine, divided

1 (12-ounce) package whole green beans, trimmed

2 tablespoons Dijon mustard

1. In a shallow dish, mix the flour with 1½ teaspoons of the rosemary. Season the chicken cutlets with salt and black pepper, then dredge in flour, shaking off excess.

2. Heat the olive oil in a large skillet over medium-high heat. Brown the chicken for 2 to 3 minutes on each side. Remove the chicken from the pan.

3. Add the garlic and ½ cup of the white wine to the pan, stirring to deglaze pan. Add the green beans and season with ½ teaspoon each of salt and black pepper. Cook for 5 minutes, stirring occasionally.

ONE-POT
NUT-FREE
DAIRY-FREE

SERVES: 4

Per Serving

Calories: 306; Total Fat: 9g;
Saturated Fat: 1g;
Carbohydrates: 18g;
Fiber: 4g; Protein: 29g

Substitution Tips:

* You may use chicken broth instead of the white wine, but do not use cooking wine.
* For a creamier sauce, add a little heavy cream with the white wine.

4. Return the chicken to the pan. Whisk the Dijon mustard into the remaining white wine, then pour the mixture over the chicken and sprinkle with 1 teaspoon minced rosemary.

5. Cover and reduce heat to medium-low. Continue cooking for about 10 minutes, or until the chicken is done and the green beans are crisp and tender. Garnish with fresh rosemary sprigs and serve.

Cuban Mojo Pork Chops and Orange Rice

PREP TIME: 10 MINUTES / MARINATE TIME: 2 TO 8 HOURS / COOK TIME: 25 MINUTES

The marinade for this pork chop skillet was adapted from the Mojo-Marinated Pork Shoulder recipe created for the film Chef, *by Chef Roy Choi. Mojo is a Cuban marinade usually made from sour oranges. In this recipe, a mix of orange and lime is used instead to help tenderize the pork and give it amazing flavor.*

Juice and zest of 2 oranges, divided

¼ cup fresh lime juice

4 garlic cloves, mined

2 tablespoons minced fresh mint leaves divided

½ teaspoon dried oregano

1 teaspoon cumin

1 teaspoon kosher salt

½ teaspoon black pepper

4 (¾-inch thick) boneless pork chops

2 tablespoons extra-virgin olive oil

1 cup white long-grain rice

2 cups chicken stock or broth

ONE-POT
NUT-FREE
DAIRY-FREE

SERVES: **4**

Per Serving

Calories: 485; Total Fat: 21g;
Saturated Fat: 6g;
Carbohydrates: 46g;
Fiber: 1g; Protein: 29g

Tip:

★ Chef Choi's original recipe calls for lots of cilantro. However, since my husband is not a fan, I made the marinade without the cilantro, and it was still delicious. If you love cilantro, toss a handful of chopped leaves into the marinade.

1. To prepare the marinade: Combine the juice of one orange with the lime juice, garlic, 1 tablespoon of the fresh mint, the dried oregano, cumin, salt, and black pepper. Pour the marinade into a resealable plastic bag with the pork chops and refrigerate for 2 to 8 hours.

2. Heat the olive oil in a large skillet over medium-high heat. Remove the pork chops, discarding the marinade, and sear them in the hot oil for 2 to 3 minutes on each side. Set aside on a plate.

3. Add the rice to the pan and stir for a couple of minutes until it begins to smell toasty. Pour in the chicken stock with the juice and zest of the remaining orange.

4. Bring to a boil, then reduce heat to low and simmer. Return the pork chops to the pan, cover with a lid, and cook for 18 to 20 minutes, until most of the liquid is absorbed. Fluff the rice, garnish with the remaining fresh mint, and serve.

Sheet Pan Sweet and Sour Chicken

PREP TIME: 10 MINUTES / COOK TIME: 25 MINUTES

No need for a wok! This meal bakes in an aluminum foil-lined sheet pan for easy cleanup. Red pepper flakes from the sweet chili sauce add a little heat to this yummy dish that you'll want to make again and again.

Cooking spray

2 skinless, boneless chicken breasts

3½ tablespoons cornstarch, divided

1 teaspoon kosher salt

½ teaspoon black pepper

2 bell peppers (red or green), seeded and cut into bite-size pieces

1 (15-ounce) can pineapple chunks, plus ⅓ cup juice

¾ cup sweet chili sauce

2 tablespoons low-sodium soy sauce

1. Preheat the oven to 450°F. Line a large rimmed baking sheet with aluminum foil and coat lightly with cooking spray.

2. Rinse the chicken and pat dry with paper towels. Cut into bite size pieces and place in a gallon-size resealable bag with 2½ tablespoons of the cornstarch, the salt, and black pepper. Shake to coat on all sides, then empty onto baking sheet along with the bell peppers. Bake for 15 minutes.

ONE-POT
EASY CLASSIC
NUT-FREE
DAIRY-FREE

SERVES: 4

Per Serving

Calories: 286; Total Fat: 3g;
Saturated Fat: 1g;
Carbohydrates: 40g;
Fiber: 2g; Protein: 21g

Substitution Tip:

* Use a fresh pineapple instead of the canned pineapple chunks, but be sure to reserve enough juice to make the sauce.

3. While the chicken is baking, make the sweet and sour sauce: Drain the pineapple and reserve ⅓ cup juice. Whisk together the pineapple juice, sweet chili sauce, soy sauce, and remaining cornstarch.

4. Remove the chicken and bell peppers from the oven and add the pineapple. Pour the sweet and sour sauce all over and stir to coat all ingredients. Return to the oven and bake for 10 more minutes.

Sloppy Joes

PREP TIME: 10 MINUTES / COOK TIME: 20 MINUTES

Use a fork—they're called "sloppy" for a reason—so you don't miss a single, tasty bite of these nostalgic sandwiches. Make a double batch to freeze for another easy meal or to repurpose into a hearty Shepherd's Pie (see page 87).

1 pound ground beef (85% lean)

¼ cup finely chopped onion

¼ cup finely chopped celery

¼ cup finely chopped green bell pepper

½ teaspoon kosher salt

½ teaspoon black pepper

½ cup Easy Barbecue Sauce with Molasses (see page 71)

4 round buns, optional

1. Crumble the ground beef into a skillet. Cook and stir over medium-high heat for 7 to 8 minutes, until the beef is no longer pink. Drain off grease.

2. Add the onion, celery, bell pepper, salt, and black pepper and continue cooking for another 3 to 5 minutes until the vegetables are soft.

3. Reduce heat to medium and stir in the barbecue sauce.

4. Simmer for about 5 minutes, or until the meat mixture reduces to your desired thickness. Serve on buns (if desired).

ONE-POT
MAKE-AHEAD
EASY CLASSIC
NUT-FREE
DAIRY-FREE

SERVES: 4

Per Serving

Calories: 294; Total Fat: 17g; Saturated Fat: 7g; Carbohydrates: 13g; Fiber: 1g; Protein: 21g

Substitution Tip:

★ Try substituting sofritto (see the sidebar, Sofritto: A Chef's Secret, on page 61) for the onion, celery, and green bell pepper in this recipe.

Use the Leftovers:

★ Make a hearty Shepherd's Pie (see page 87) with my Sour Cream Mashed Potatoes (see page 111) and Sloppy Joes.

Spaghetti Squash Florentine

Skip the pasta in this rich yet delicate Florentine casserole. This recipe saves loads of carbs and adds a heap of nutrients by using spaghetti squash noodles, which can be substituted in many pasta dishes or simply served topped with marinara sauce.

1 (3-pound) spaghetti squash

½ cup water

1 tablespoon extra-virgin olive oil

4 cups chopped fresh spinach

½ red bell pepper, seeded and diced

1 garlic clove, minced

1 teaspoon kosher salt

½ teaspoon black pepper

Dash nutmeg

8 ounces low-fat cream cheese

Cooking spray

¼ cup freshly grated Parmesan cheese

MAKE-AHEAD
NUT-FREE
GLUTEN-FREE
VEGETARIAN

SERVES: 4

Per Serving

Calories: 341; Total Fat: 21g;
Saturated Fat: 12g;
Carbohydrates: 24g;
Fiber: 1g; Protein: 8g

1. Preheat the oven to 400°F. Slice the spaghetti squash in half lengthwise and scoop out the seeds. Place the two squash halves cut-side down in a glass baking dish and add ½ cup of water. Bake for 30 minutes.

2. Remove the squash from the oven, flip over, and let cool for 5 to 10 minutes. Use a fork to gently shred the pulp inside the squash.

Continued ▶

3. While the squash is baking, heat the olive oil in a large skillet over medium heat. Add the chopped spinach, bell pepper, garlic, salt, black pepper, and nutmeg. Sauté just until the spinach is wilted. Add the cream cheese and stir gently until melted. Stir the spaghetti squash into the cooked spinach until combined.

4. Lightly coat a casserole dish with cooking spray and pour the squash mixture into the dish. Top with the Parmesan cheese and bake immediately, or cover and refrigerate to bake at a later time.

5. To bake, preheat the oven to 375°F. Cook for about 30 minutes, or until bubbly and the cheese is lightly browned.

Easy Barbecue Sauce with Molasses

Tangy and sweet with a little kick, this easy barbecue sauce is extremely versatile. Use it to baste grilled chicken or pork ribs, as the base for a BBQ chicken pizza, or simply as a dipping sauce for fried chicken tenders.

1 cup raw apple cider vinegar

1 cup ketchup

⅔ cup molasses

4 tablespoons yellow mustard

4 tablespoons brown sugar

2 teaspoons kosher salt

2 teaspoons black pepper, coarse ground or freshly ground

1 teaspoon chili powder

1. Add all the ingredients to a heavy saucepan and bring to a boil over medium heat, stirring until the brown sugar dissolves.

2. Reduce heat to low and simmer for 20 to 30 minutes, or until desired thickness is achieved.

3. Serve warm or cool completely and refrigerate for later use.

ONE-POT
NUT-FREE
DAIRY-FREE
VEGAN

YIELDS 2½ CUPS

Per Serving (¼ cup)

Calories: 110; Total Fat: 0g; Saturated Fat: 0g; Carbohydrates: 27g; Fiber: 0g; Protein: 1g

Use the Leftovers:

★ Use this versatile recipe to make a tasty BBQ Pork Sandwich with Pickled Red Onions (page 86).

Substitution Tip:

★ You may use either raw or filtered apple cider vinegar. Raw vinegar is less processed and has more flavor complexity.

Classic Marinara Sauce

The redder and riper the tomatoes, the more amazing this sauce becomes as it simmers. Plan to double the recipe and save some for my Spinach-Stuffed Jumbo Shells (page 89).

2 quarts water

2½ pounds Roma tomatoes

½ cup yellow onion, diced

¼ cup extra-virgin olive oil

4 garlic cloves, chopped

1 teaspoon dried oregano

Kosher salt, optional

¼ cup minced fresh basil

1. Bring 2 quarts of water to a boil. Immediately remove from heat and submerge the tomatoes in the hot water for 5 minutes.

2. In the meantime, add the onions and olive oil to a large saucepan. Cook over medium-low heat for 5 to 10 minutes, or until onions start to caramelize. Add the garlic to the pan and cook for another minute until the garlic is fragrant.

3. Drain the tomatoes and run cool water over them until they are cool enough to handle. Use a small paring knife to gently peel skin away from the flesh of the tomatoes.

ONE-POT
EASY CLASSIC
NUT-FREE
SOY-FREE
VEGAN

YIELDS **3 CUPS**

Per Serving (½ cup)

Calories: 114; Total Fat: 9g;
Saturated Fat: 1g;
Carbohydrates: 9g;
Fiber: 3g; Protein: 2g

Tip:

★ If you can't find fresh Roma tomatoes, use 2 (28-ounce) cans of quality whole tomatoes instead.

4. Use your hands to crush the tomatoes, then add them to the saucepan with the oregano. Bring to a boil, then reduce heat to a slow simmer. Cook for 30 minutes, stirring occasionally with a wooden spoon to further crush the tomatoes against side of the pan.

5. Season with salt (if desired). Remove from heat and stir in the basil. Serve over your favorite pasta or zucchini noodles. Let the sauce cool before storing in your refrigerator.

Tex-Mex Stuffed Bell Peppers

PREP TIME: 15 MINUTES / COOK TIME: 20 MINUTES

The spicy chili in these stuffed peppers is made with ground turkey, which is leaner and has fewer calories than beef. The spice mix sautéed with the turkey gives it a nice caramel color and beautiful flavor, so no one will be the wiser!

Cooking spray

3 large bell peppers (red, yellow, or green)

1 tablespoon extra-virgin olive oil

½ large onion, diced

1 pound ground turkey

1 tablespoon chili powder

1 teaspoon ground cumin

1 teaspoon smoked paprika

1 teaspoon kosher salt

½ teaspoon black pepper

½ teaspoon coriander

1 (10-ounce) can diced tomatoes and green chiles

½ cup shredded Cheddar cheese

1. Preheat the oven to 450°F. Line a baking sheet with aluminum foil and spray lightly with cooking spray. Cut the bell peppers in half from top to bottom and remove the seeds. Place on the baking sheet, cut-side up, and salt the inside. Bake for 2 to 3 minutes, then drain off any liquid and return to baking sheet.

2. Heat 1 tablespoon of the olive oil in a large skillet over medium-high heat. Add the onion and ground turkey and cook for 5 minutes, stirring frequently. Drain off grease.

MAKE-AHEAD
NUT-FREE
GLUTEN-FREE
SOY-FREE

SERVES: **5**

Per Serving

Calories: 295; Total Fat: 17g;
Saturated Fat: 5g;
Carbohydrates: 11g;
Fiber: 3g; Protein: 29g

Tips:

★ Dice up leftover bell pepper and put it in a resealable freezer bag to freeze for later use.

★ Bell peppers release liquid as they cook, so prebaking them for a few minutes helps keep the stuffed peppers from getting watery. Just be sure to avoid overcooking them before stuffing so you don't end up with withered stuffed peppers.

3. Sprinkle the chili powder, cumin, smoked paprika, salt, black pepper, and coriander on top of the meat and stir until coated. Add the diced tomatoes and green chiles and continue cooking for 2 to 3 minutes, or until any moisture is absorbed.

4. Spoon the turkey chili into the bell pepper cups. Depending on the size of the peppers, you will have enough chili to fill 5 or 6 peppers. Top with Cheddar cheese, bake for 20 minutes, and serve.

Cold Shrimp Salad

This seafood salad doesn't get any easier. Just toss the shrimp with crunchy celery and dress it with a lemon and dill infused low-fat mayo. Dinner is served.

1 pound cooked and peeled shrimp (baby shrimp or cocktail shrimp from the seafood counter)

2 green onions, diced

½ cup finely diced celery

¼ cup low-fat mayonnaise

1 tablespoon fresh lemon juice

1 teaspoon lemon zest

½ teaspoon dill weed (or 1 teaspoon snipped fresh dill)

½ teaspoon kosher salt

½ teaspoon freshly ground black pepper

NO-COOK
NUT-FREE
DAIRY-FREE

SERVES: **4**

Per Serving

Calories: 147; Total Fat: 4g;
Saturated Fat: 1g;
Carbohydrates: 3g;
Fiber: 1g; Protein: 25g

1. Rinse and drain the shrimp well. Place the shrimp in a bowl with the green onions and celery and toss gently. If using cocktail-size shrimp, roughly chop them first.

2. Whisk together the mayonnaise, lemon juice, lemon zest, dill weed, salt, and black pepper. Pour the mixture over the shrimp and stir until combined. Garnish with additional freshly ground black pepper (if desired) and serve immediately, or chill on a lettuce-lined plate first to allow the flavors to meld.

Arugula Salad Pizzas

PREP TIME: 15 MINUTES

Skip the oven for this unique take on pizza with fresh veggies. Use either pita bread or personal-size naan and pile on baby arugula, cherry tomatoes, and a lovely mustard vinaigrette.

2 tablespoons red wine vinegar

1 tablespoon Dijon mustard (or stone-ground Dijon mustard)

1 garlic clove, minced

4 tablespoons extra-virgin olive oil

¼ teaspoon kosher salt

¼ teaspoon freshly ground black pepper

5 cups baby arugula

4 pita bread rounds or personal size naan, warmed or toasted

1 pint cherry or grape tomatoes, quartered

2 tablespoons freshly grated Parmesan cheese

NO-COOK
NUT-FREE
GLUTEN-FREE
VEGETARIAN

SERVES: 4

Per Serving

Calories: 237; Total Fat: 16g; Saturated Fat: 3g; Carbohydrates: 22g; Fiber: 3g; Protein: 5g

1. To make the dressing: Whisk together the red wine vinegar, Dijon mustard, garlic, olive oil, salt, and black pepper in a small bowl until emulsified.

2. Place the arugula in a large bowl and drizzle the dressing on top, tossing to coat.

3. Equally divide the arugula salad on top of the pita bread rounds. Sprinkle each with the tomatoes and Parmesan cheese.

Chopped Kale and Salami Salad with Honey Dijon Vinaigrette

PREP TIME: 15 MINUTES

The Tavern Restaurant in Nashville, Tennessee, has a superb kale salad that's chopped so fine it's almost the consistency of tabbouleh. This recipe follows the same technique, resulting in an easy-to-eat salad that doesn't need to be drowned in dressing. Here, the sweetness in the honey Dijon vinaigrette balances the saltiness of the salami and cheese.

5 cups kale

2 tablespoons white wine vinegar

2 tablespoons honey

1 tablespoon Dijon mustard

¼ cup extra-virgin olive oil

¼ teaspoon sea salt, optional

Freshly ground black pepper, optional

1 cup Italian dry-cured salami, diced

8 ounces aged sharp white Cheddar cheese, cut into small cubes

1. Remove the stems from the kale leaves, rinse, and spin dry in a salad spinner. Chop into small pieces (see Tip).

2. Whisk together the white wine vinegar, honey, and Dijon mustard. Slowly add the olive oil while whisking vigorously until emulsified. Season with salt and black pepper (if desired).

3. Toss the kale, salami, and Cheddar cheese with enough vinaigrette to lightly coat the greens. Garnish with freshly ground black pepper and serve.

NO-COOK
NUT-FREE

SERVES: 4

Per Serving

Calories: 429; Total Fat: 33g; Saturated Fat: 12g; Carbohydrates: 18g; Fiber: 1g; Protein: 15g

Tip:

★ Place the kale in a food processor and pulse a few times to quickly chop it into small, bite size pieces.

Flavor Swaps:

★ Try freshly shaved Parmesan cheese instead of the sharp white Cheddar cheese.
★ If you have them on hand, toss in any olives, pepperoncini, artichoke hearts, grape tomatoes, or cucumber.

Turkey Pesto Focaccia Sandwiches

PREP TIME: 10 MINUTES

If you've never made pesto, you've been missing out. One perk to making it at home is taking a big whiff of the fresh basil leaves before you blend them up—it's like aromatherapy! Besides, fresh pesto adds a wonderful Italian flavor to this easy gourmet sandwich.

1 tablespoon toasted pine nuts or walnuts

1 garlic clove

1 cup fresh basil leaves, removed from stems

¼ cup extra-virgin olive oil

¼ cup freshly grated Parmesan cheese

¼ teaspoon sea salt, plus more for seasoning

1 (8-inch) round focaccia bread, halved horizontally

¼ pound smoked deli turkey

1 small tomato, thinly sliced

Freshly ground black pepper

1. Place the pine nuts and garlic in a food processor and pulse until chopped. Add the basil leaves and pulse until chopped to desired consistency.

2. Pour the olive oil into the food processor chute while blending on low to combine; add more olive oil if you desire. Stir in the Parmesan cheese and sea salt.

3. Spread the pesto on one cut side of the focaccia. Layer the smoked turkey and tomatoes on top of the pesto and sprinkle with sea salt and freshly ground black pepper. Spread the pesto on the other piece of focaccia and finish building the sandwich. Cut into quarters and serve.

NO-COOK

SERVES: 4

Per Serving

Calories: 310; Total Fat: 19g;
Saturated Fat: 3g;
Carbohydrates: 25g;
Fiber: 1g; Protein: 12g

Tips:

* Make extra pesto and save for later. Put extra pesto in a jar and drizzle a layer of olive oil on top. Refrigerate for up to 3 days in a sealed jar.
* Consider adding other fresh ingredients to your sandwich like arugula, thinly sliced red onions, or sliced fresh mozzarella.

Pan-Seared New York Strip

PREP TIME: 30 MINUTES / COOK TIME: 15 MINUTES

If you've been wondering how to prepare a restaurant-quality steak without a grill, stove-to-oven cast iron cooking is the answer! No fancy marinades required; this recipe will give you perfectly cooked steaks every time.

4 (1-inch to 1½-inch thick cuts) New York strip steaks, fat trimmed

Sea salt

Freshly ground black pepper

1½ cups mushrooms, sliced

1 garlic clove, sliced

4 tablespoons unsalted butter

EASY CLASSIC
NUT-FREE
GLUTEN-FREE
DAIRY-FREE
SOY-FREE

SERVES: 4

Per Serving

Calories: 335; Total Fat: 18g; Saturated Fat: 7g; Carbohydrates: 1g; Fiber: 0g; Protein: 36g

1. Remove the steaks from refrigerator 30 minutes before cooking to bring them down to room temperature.

2. Preheat the oven to 400°F.

3. Heat a large cast-iron skillet over medium-high heat until it is hot, but not smoking.

4. While the skillet is heating up, season both sides of the steak with sea salt and black pepper. Drizzle the steaks with olive oil and gently rub in the salt and pepper.

5. Place the seasoned steaks into the hot skillet and cook for 2 to 3 minutes, without turning, to get a nice sear. Turn the steaks using tongs and sear the other side for another 2 to 3 minutes.

6. Remove the cast-iron skillet from the heat and add the mushrooms, garlic, and butter. Immediately place skillet in the preheated oven and roast for 4 to 7 minutes, or until the desired temperature is reached. Use touch test (see Tip), or use a digital thermometer to gauge the steaks' temperature.

7. Remove the steaks from the oven and tent with foil, allowing the steaks to rest for a couple of minutes before serving.

Tip:

* You can gently press tongs into the cooked steak to determine its doneness with this touch test guide. To be totally accurate, use a quick-read digital thermometer.
  + RARE (120°F): cool, bright red center and soft to the touch
  + MEDIUM RARE (130°F): warm, red center and beginning to firm up with red juices
  + MEDIUM (145°F to 155°F): slightly pink center, completely firm with brown juices
  + WELL DONE (155°F to 160°F): very little or no pink, firm to the touch

Crispy Oven-Fried Fish Sticks

PREP TIME: 15 MINUTES / COOK TIME: 20 MINUTES

This healthy, oven-baked fish recipe calls for a one-two-three dredging process, resulting in a crunchy coating without deep frying or added calories.

4 tilapia filets (or other mild white fish)

⅔ cup flour

1 teaspoon lemon zest (save the rest of the lemon to squeeze on the baked fish)

½ teaspoon salt

½ teaspoon freshly ground black pepper

1½ cups panko breadcrumbs

2 eggs, beaten

2 tablespoons extra-virgin olive oil

1. Preheat the oven to 375°F. Line a baking sheet with parchment paper.

2. Cut each filet into 4 smaller pieces, like fish sticks.

3. Set up a dredging station with three shallow dishes: one for the flour, lemon zest, salt, and black pepper; one for the beaten eggs; and one for the panko breadcrumbs.

4. To coat the fish, first dredge each piece in the flour mixture, then dip into the egg, and finally dredge in the panko, making sure the fish is coated on all sides. Place on the lined baking sheet. Repeat this for each piece of fish.

5. Drizzle the tops of the breaded fish with olive oil. Bake for about 20 minutes, or until fish flakes easily with a fork. Serve immediately with a squeeze of lemon and tartar sauce or malt vinegar.

EASY CLASSIC
NUT-FREE
DAIRY-FREE

SERVES: **4**

Per Serving

Calories: 332; Total Fat: 13g; Saturated Fat: 2g; Carbohydrates: 28g; Fiber: 2g; Protein: 28g

Tip:

* For a more golden crust, once the fish is done, increase the heat and place the fish under the broiler for a couple of minutes. Watch carefully to avoid burning.

Slow Cooker Beef Pot Roast with Mushrooms

PREP TIME: 30 MINUTES / COOK TIME: 8 HOURS

Slow cooking all day results in the most succulent beef pot roast you've ever tasted! This roast is delicious served over rice, noodles, or my Sour Cream Mashed Potatoes (see page 111). Be sure to save the leftovers for sandwiches later in the week.

Cooking spray

1 large onion, cut into wedges

3 cups sliced mushrooms

3 pounds beef shoulder roast

2 teaspoons kosher salt

1 teaspoon black pepper, coarse ground or freshly ground

2 tablespoons extra-virgin olive oil

1 garlic clove, minced

3 cups beef broth

¼ cup Worcestershire sauce

1. Lightly coat the bottom of a slow cooker with cooking spray. Add the onion wedges and mushrooms to the bottom of the slow cooker.

2. Season the roast on all sides with salt and black pepper, pressing into the meat.

3. Heat the olive oil in a large skillet over medium-high heat. Add the garlic and stir until fragrant.

ONE-POT
NUT-FREE
DAIRY-FREE

SERVES: **8 TO 10**

Per Serving

Calories: 321; Total Fat: 16g;
Saturated Fat: 4g;
Carbohydrates: 5g;
Fiber: 1g; Protein: 37g

Use the Leftovers:

* Make my lip-smacking Cold Roast Beef Sandwich with Horseradish Aioli (see page 55).

Continued ▷

4. Sear the roast in the hot oil on all sides, then add it to the slow cooker, leaving behind any burnt pieces of garlic. Add the beef broth and Worcestershire sauce.

5. Cook on low for 8 hours. Remove the roast to a cutting board and let it rest for 10 to 15 minutes before carving.

6. Serve sliced or shredded roast *au jus*. If you prefer a thicker gravy, make a slurry of ¼ cup of beef liquid and ¼ cup cornstarch, then stir it into the juices in slow cooker and cook for a few more minutes until thickened.

Tip:

★ Searing the beef roast before adding it to the slow cooker will caramelize the surface and give the recipe a rich flavor. You can coat the meat in flour before browning it to add body to the gravy, but I prefer to add cornstarch for thickening at the end of cooking—less mess and just as effective.

Sunday Roast Chicken

PREP TIME: 15 MINUTES / COOK TIME: 2 HOURS

Moist and juicy Sunday chicken just like Grandma used to make! The ingredient list may look long, but all you really need for this dinner is a chicken, fresh basil, and a few spices out of your pantry.

1 (6-to 7-pound) whole roasting chicken

1 tablespoon minced fresh basil

1 tablespoon kosher salt

2 teaspoons sugar

½ teaspoon freshly ground black pepper

¼ teaspoon garlic powder

¼ teaspoon onion powder

¼ teaspoon paprika

½ teaspoon fresh lemon juice

2 tablespoons extra-virgin olive oil

ONE-POT
NUT-FREE
DAIRY-FREE
SOY-FREE

SERVES: 6

Per Serving

Calories: 865; Total Fat: 62g;
Saturated Fat: 17g;
Carbohydrates: 2g;
Fiber: 0g; Protein: 71g

Tips:

* A variety of root vegetables like potatoes, carrots, onions, or parsnips can be roasted along with the chicken. Nestle them around the bird, and the juices will season and flavor them as the chicken roasts.
* Unless you're adding vegetables to the pan, the chicken may be placed on a rack inside the pan, but it is not really necessary.

1. Preheat the oven to 350°F.

2. Remove all parts from the chicken cavity and discard. Rinse the chicken under cool water inside and out. Pat dry with paper towels and tie the legs together with cooking twine. Place the chicken in a large roasting pan.

3. To make the rub: Mix together the basil, salt, sugar, black pepper, garlic powder, onion powder, paprika, lemon juice, and olive oil. Apply the rub liberally all over the chicken. Bake uncovered for 2 hours.

4. Allow to cool slightly before carving or removing meat from the bone.

BBQ Pork Sandwich with Pickled Red Onions

PREP TIME: 5 MINUTES / COOK TIME: 25 MINUTES

You'll be amazed at the flavor boost the quick pickled red onions add when paired with take-out leftovers or store-bought pulled pork and my Easy Barbecue Sauce with Molasses.

1 large red onion, thinly sliced and separated into rings

3 tablespoons raw apple cider vinegar

1 teaspoon sugar

¼ teaspoon kosher salt

1 cup Easy Barbecue Sauce with Molasses (see page 71)

1 pound pulled pork

4 large hamburger buns

1. To make the pickled red onions: Up to an hour before serving, add the red onions to a shallow bowl. Combine the apple cider vinegar, sugar, and salt; pour over the onions, and stir to coat. Allow to sit at room temperature at least 30 minutes (or up to an hour), stirring occasionally to make sure all the onions are moistened.

2. Heat the barbecue sauce in the microwave.

3. Divide the pulled pork between hamburger buns, about 4 ounces per serving. Drizzle with the barbecue sauce and top with a pile of pickled red onions.

REINVENTION
NUT-FREE
DAIRY-FREE

SERVES: **4**

Per Serving

Calories: 378; Total Fat: 7g; Saturated Fat: 2g; Carbohydrates: 61g; Fiber: 2g; Protein: 20g

Flavor Swap:
* This sandwich is just as tasty with pulled smoked chicken.

Tips:
* To make red onions milder, pour 2 cups of boiling water over the rings and drain immediately in a colander. Proceed with the pickling instructions.
* Store pickled red onions tightly covered in the refrigerator for 3 to 4 days.

Shepherd's Pie

PREP TIME: 15 MINUTES / COOK TIME: 15 MINUTES

Nothing is more comforting than this hearty and classic dish with its beefy filling and creamy, cheesy potato topping. Use leftovers from recipes in this cookbook, and you can have this dinner on the table in half the normal time.

Cooking spray

1 cup fresh mushrooms, sliced

1 teaspoon extra-virgin olive oil

1 garlic clove, minced

2½ to 3 cups meat from Sloppy Joes (see page 68)

2 cups frozen peas and carrots, thawed

1 tablespoon beef bouillon granules

2½ to 3 cups Sour Cream Mashed Potatoes (see page 111)

1 tablespoon fresh thyme leaves

1 cup shredded Cheddar cheese

MAKE-AHEAD
EASY CLASSIC
REINVENTION
NUT-FREE

SERVES: 4

Per Serving

Calories: 502; Total Fat: 22g;
Saturated Fat: 11g;
Carbohydrates: 51g;
Fiber: 6g; Protein: 28g

1. Preheat the oven to 400°F. Lightly coat a 2-quart casserole dish with cooking spray.

2. In a large skillet over medium heat, sauté the sliced mushrooms in the olive oil for about 5 minutes, until tender. Add the garlic and cook for about a minute, until fragrant.

3. To the skillet, add the Sloppy Joe meat, peas and carrots, and beef bouillon granules. Cook and stir until heated through. Transfer this mixture to the prepared casserole dish.

Continued ▶

4. Heat the mashed potatoes in the microwave until they are soft enough to stir and spread. Stir in the thyme leaves. Spoon the potatoes into the casserole dish and smooth with the back of spoon until all meat is covered.

5. Sprinkle evenly with the Cheddar cheese and bake for about 15 minutes, or until hot and bubbly. Let stand for 5 minutes before serving.

Tip:

*   Make this casserole ahead, freeze it, and save it for a busy week. Assemble the casserole through step 4, then cover it tightly with aluminum foil and store it in the freezer for up to a month. To serve, let it thaw in the refrigerator for 24 hours. Sprinkle with 1 cup Cheddar cheese and bake at 400°F for about 40 minutes, or until heated through. Cover with aluminum foil after 25 minutes of baking to keep the Shepherd's Pie from getting overly browned.

Spinach-Stuffed Jumbo Shells

PREP TIME: 15 MINUTES / COOK TIME: 1 HOUR

No need to pre-boil the shells or cook the spinach before assembling this satisfying cheesy baked Italian dish, featuring my homemade Classic Marinara Sauce.

1 cup chopped fresh spinach

2 cups shredded mozzarella cheese, divided

1 (15-ounce) container whole milk ricotta cheese

½ teaspoon kosher salt

Freshly ground black pepper

3 cups Classic Marinara Sauce (see page 72)

1 (8-ounce) package jumbo pasta shells (20 to 24 shells)

1. Preheat the oven to 350°F.

2. In a bowl, combine the spinach with 1 cup of the mozzarella, ricotta, salt, and black pepper.

3. Spread ½ cup of the marinara sauce on the bottom of a 9-by-13-inch glass baking dish.

4. Stuff the pasta shells with the spinach and cheese mixture. Place them in the dish cheese-side up. Spoon the remaining marinara sauce on top, completely covering the pasta. Cover with foil and bake for 1 hour.

5. Uncover and sprinkle with the remaining mozzarella. Bake for about 10 more minutes, or until cheese is melted and bubbly.

REINVENTION
NUT-FREE
VEGETARIAN

SERVES: 5

Per Serving

Calories: 607; Total Fat: 28g;
Saturated Fat: 16g;
Carbohydrates: 56g;
Fiber: 5g; Protein: 34g

Substitution Tip:

* You can use manicotti instead of shells. Place cheese and spinach mixture into a large resealable plastic bag. Cut a hole in one corner and pipe the filling into the shells.

Baja Fish Tacos

PREP TIME: 15 MINUTES / COOK TIME: 15 MINUTES

Spicy fish, tangy cabbage slaw, and sweet mango salsa combine for a great flavor profile in these Baja Fish Tacos. The ground cinnamon in the fish rub may be unexpected, but it is quite pleasing.

For the cabbage slaw:
2 cups finely shredded cabbage

½ tablespoon extra-virgin olive oil

½ tablespoon red wine vinegar

Salt

Freshly ground black pepper

For the fish rub:
1 teaspoon chili powder

1 teaspoon cumin

1 teaspoon kosher salt

½ teaspoon red cayenne pepper

½ teaspoon ground cinnamon

For the fish tacos:
Cooking Spray

4 tilapia fillets

Flour or corn tortillas

1 cup Mango Salsa (see page 130)

1. Preheat the oven to 400°F.

2. To make the cabbage slaw: Toss the cabbage with the olive oil and red wine vinegar. Season with salt and black pepper to taste. Refrigerate until ready to use.

REINVENTION
NUT-FREE
DAIRY-FREE

SERVES: 4

Per Serving
Calories: 232; Total Fat: 6g; Saturated Fat: 1g; Carbohydrates: 24g; Fiber: 3g; Protein: 23g

Tips:
* For grilling, heat the grill to medium-high heat. Cook the fish on a lightly oiled grill pan for 6 to 7 minutes on each side.
* Flavor some low-fat sour cream with a little lime juice, fresh cilantro, and a sprinkle of salt and pepper for another taco topping option.

Continued ▷

3. To make the fish rub: Mix together the spices for the rub.

4. Line a baking sheet with aluminum foil lightly coated with cooking spray.

5. Rinse the tilapia and pat dry with paper towels. Sprinkle the fish rub over both sides of the fillets, lightly rubbing into the fish.

6. Bake the fish for 12 to 15 minutes, or until the fish flakes easily with a fork.

7. Break the filets into small pieces and serve on warmed flour or corn tortillas with the salsa.

Roasted Brussels Sprouts with
Pancetta and Pecans, page 109

CHAPTER FIVE

Veggies & Sides

Every delicious entrée deserves an equally delicious accompaniment. In this chapter, you'll find plenty of easy side dishes to complement any main course—many of which can be prepared in under 30 minutes. Roasted vegetable recipes, like Brussels Sprouts with Pancetta and Pecans or Perfectly Roasted Asparagus, are not only quick and easy to prepare, they're also elegant enough to accompany a nice steak dinner. In addition, included are several tasty salads and other delicious classics that will remind you of dining at Grandma's dinner table, like my Sour Cream Mashed Potatoes and Orange-Kissed Carrots.

Love your veggies!

"Eat your veggies!" is probably being announced around someone's dinner table right now as you're reading this sentence. For years, it seemed that my own children wouldn't touch anything green that I put on their plates without a protest, especially if those vegetables sat alongside a serving of macaroni and cheese. Thankfully, they outgrew their veggie aversion over time and even came to love eating all kinds of vegetables like Brussels sprouts and asparagus.

Unlike me, my children didn't experience dirty hands from harvesting potatoes or getting itchy from picking okra and green beans on summer breaks. During their childhood, we never lived in a place that was suitable for a vegetable garden, which made visiting my parents' farm a great learning experience for my kids. My dad loved showing us how the garden was growing, pointing out the rows of tomatoes and cabbages, and loading us down with bags of fresh produce.

Now, my girls would tell you that homegrown tomatoes indeed taste the very best and nothing compares with eating a warm juicy strawberry picked fresh from the vine. Everyone should experience this at least once!

Today, more people are genuinely interested in knowing where their food comes from and often choose to purchase organic vegetables that were grown free of synthetic fertilizers and pesticides. In many urban areas, people can participate in community gardening. Similarly, innovative school-sponsored gardens give children a real hands-on lesson about growing healthy foods. The sprouting emphasis is on cultivating an ecosystem that sustains and nourishes plants and, ultimately, improves the soil.

It may not always seem practical to purchase organic vegetables, but, in some instances, it is a smart choice (see The Dirty Dozen™ and the Clean Fifteen™ on page 161). Either way, follow these U.S. Food and Drug Administration guidelines[3]

---

[3] Glenda Lewis, "7 Tips for Cleaning Fruits, Vegetables," FDA Consumer Updates, *U.S. Food & Drug Administration*, June 10, 2018.

when purchasing and storing produce at home to help protect your family against contamination:

* Choose fruits and vegetables that are not bruised or damaged.
* Make sure precut veggies or fruits are either refrigerated or on ice in the store (and be sure to refrigerate them at home).
* Wash your hands before and after preparing fresh produce.
* Rinse and gently rub produce under plain running water before peeling it—do not use soap—and dry it with a clean cloth or paper towel.
* Always remove the outermost leaves from lettuce or cabbages.
* Store perishable produce in the refrigerator at or below 40°F.

Vegetables are an important source of nutrients, dietary fiber, and vitamins, and, when part of an overall diet, they can help reduce cholesterol levels and may lower risk of heart disease. All of that sounds like a good enough reason to me to eat your veggies.

Perfectly Roasted Asparagus

The secret to perfectly roasted asparagus is choosing the right size stalks and avoiding over-cooking. Spears that are too skinny will shrivel up, and really large asparagus stalks tend to be tough. The best choice for tender roasted asparagus is a medium-size stalk, and the optimal baking time is right around 12 minutes.

30 to 40 medium-size asparagus spears, trimmed

1½ tablespoons extra-virgin olive oil

½ teaspoon sea salt

½ teaspoon freshly ground black pepper

1. Preheat the oven to 400°F. Rinse and dry the asparagus; break off the tough end of the stems.

2. Place the asparagus on a rimmed baking sheet and toss with the olive oil. Sprinkle with salt and black pepper and bake for 12 minutes. Serve immediately.

Flavor Swaps:

* Roasted asparagus is delicious all on its own just out of the oven, but you may wish to enhance the flavor with one of these variations:
  + A drizzle of traditional aged balsamic vinegar and shaved Parmesan cheese.
  + Stir together ¼ teaspoon sesame oil and a tablespoon or two of soy sauce, drizzle on top and sprinkle with toasted sesame seeds.
  + Melt a couple tablespoons of butter until it is golden brown and stir in equal amounts of soy sauce and balsamic vinegar to drizzle over roasted asparagus.

ONE-POT
NUT-FREE
GLUTEN-FREE
SOY-FREE
VEGAN

SERVES: **6**

Per Serving

Calories: 46; Total Fat: 4g;
Saturated Fat: 1g;
Carbohydrates: 3g;
Fiber: 2g; Protein: 2g

Use the Leftovers:

* Use this to make my refreshing Lemon-Basil Potato Salad (page 112).

Mexican Zucchini (*Calabacitas*)

Mexican zucchini (aka calabacitas) are a light green variety of zucchini squash, but this garden-fresh side is delicious when made with the dark green variety of zucchini as well.

1 tablespoon extra-virgin olive oil

½ cup diced onion

1 jalapeño pepper, seeded and diced

1 garlic clove, minced

2 medium Mexican zucchini, cubed

1 cup grape tomatoes, halved

Kosher salt

Freshly ground black pepper

1. Heat a tablespoon of olive oil in a large skillet over medium-high heat. Add the onion and jalapeño pepper and cook for 4 to 5 minutes, until tender. Add the garlic and cook for about 30 seconds, until fragrant.

2. Add the zucchini and tomatoes. Continue cooking for 4 to 5 minutes, until tender. DO NOT overcook—zucchini cooks quickly and can become mushy if left on heat for too long. Season with salt and black pepper and serve.

ONE-POT
NUT-FREE
GLUTEN-FREE
SOY-FREE
VEGAN

SERVES: **6**

Per Serving

Calories: 41; Total Fat: 3g; Saturated Fat: 0g; Carbohydrates: 5g; Fiber: 1g; Protein: 1g

Flavor Swaps:

★ Serve with crumbled queso fresco or cotija cheese on top or garnish with chopped cilantro to give it an authentic Mexican flavor.

★ Add a couple of ears of fresh, cut-off corn and season with chili powder and cumin to transform this dish into a Mexican succotash.

Southern Succotash

Succotash is basically fried corn cooked with bacon, lima beans, and tomatoes. This classic Southern dish, adapted from recipes of the indigenous people of New England, is a great accompaniment to grilled or fried catfish or chicken.

2 slices bacon

½ sweet onion, chopped

4 ears corn, cut off cob

1 garlic clove, minced

1½ cups frozen baby lima beans, thawed

1 cup grape (or cherry) tomatoes, halved

1 teaspoon kosher salt

½ teaspoon freshly ground black pepper

2 teaspoons fresh thyme leaves

ONE-POT
NUT-FREE
GLUTEN-FREE
DAIRY-FREE
SOY-FREE

SERVES: **4**

Per Serving

Calories: 182; Total Fat: 5g; Saturated Fat: 2g; Carbohydrates: 28g; Fiber: 5g; Protein: 9g

Flavor Swap:

∗ Freshly diced okra may be substituted for the lima beans.

1. Cook the bacon in a large skillet over medium heat until crisp. Remove the bacon from the pan to a paper towel-lined plate and pour off all but two tablespoons of grease from the pan.

2. Sauté the onion for about 5 minutes, or until translucent. Stir in the corn and garlic. Cook for another 5 to 6 minutes, or until the corn is tender.

3. Add the lima beans, tomatoes, salt, and black pepper. Continue cooking for 5 more minutes, stirring occasionally. Crumble the bacon into smaller pieces. Stir it in to the skillet with the fresh thyme leaves.

Creamed Maple Butternut Squash

PREP TIME: 15 MINUTES / COOK TIME: 25 MINUTES

Instead of boiling butternut squash, roasting it brings out its natural sweetness. Prepping and roasting squash ahead of time makes whipping up this dish go more quickly.

4 cups butternut squash, peeled and cut into 1-inch cubes (see Tip)

2 tablespoons extra-virgin olive oil

1 teaspoon kosher salt, plus more

1 teaspoon freshly ground black pepper

1 teaspoon paprika

1 tablespoon unsalted butter

¼ cup milk (or cream)

2 tablespoons maple syrup

1 teaspoon ground cinnamon

MAKE-AHEAD
NUT-FREE
GLUTEN-FREE
VEGETARIAN

SERVES: **6**

Per Serving

Calories: 124; Total Fat: 3g; Saturated Fat: 2g; Carbohydrates: 24g; Fiber: 3g; Protein: 2g

1. Preheat the oven to 400°F. On a baking sheet, toss the squash with the olive oil, salt, black pepper, and paprika. Bake for 25 minutes, turning midway. Transfer to a large, heat-safe bowl.

2. Using a hand-held mixer or potato masher, cream the butternut squash. Add the butter and milk, and continue mixing until desired consistency is reached (a few lumps are fine).

3. Stir in the maple syrup, cinnamon, and more salt (if desired) and serve.

Tip:

* To peel a butternut squash, use a fork to pierce the skin in several places. Microwave on high for two minutes. Cut off the ends and slice off the neck section. Lay the neck section flat on a cutting board and peel down the sides, then slice and cube. Cut the remaining section in half vertically to spoon out the seeds. Again, peel, slice, and cube.

Scalloped Cauliflower

PREP TIME: 5 MINUTES / COOK TIME: 40 MINUTES

This recipe takes tender steamed cauliflower and bakes it in a creamy cheese sauce to make a tasty side dish for any meal.

3 tablespoons unsalted butter, plus 1 teaspoon for greasing

1 head cauliflower, broken into florets (about 5 to 6 cups)

2 teaspoons kosher salt, divided

Water

3 tablespoons all-purpose flour

¼ teaspoon black pepper

¼ teaspoon nutmeg

1 cup milk

1½ cups shredded Swiss cheese, divided

½ teaspoon paprika

1. Preheat the oven to 375°F. Lightly grease an 11-by-7-inch glass baking dish with 1 teaspoon of butter.

2. In a large pot, add the cauliflower, 1 teaspoon of salt, and enough water to cover. Bring to a boil over medium-high heat and cook for 5 to 6 minutes, until tender. Remove from heat and drain.

3. In a heavy saucepan, melt 3 tablespoons of the unsalted butter with the flour over medium-high. Cook and stir for 2 minutes. Add the remaining salt, black pepper, and nutmeg, then slowly whisk in the milk and cook another 2 minutes, or until thickened.

MAKE-AHEAD
NUT-FREE
GLUTEN-FREE
SOY-FREE
VEGETARIAN

SERVES: 6

Per Serving

Calories: 146; Total Fat: 11g; Saturated Fat: 7g; Carbohydrates: 7g; Fiber: 1g; Protein: 6g

Flavor Swaps:

* Instead of Swiss, try using Gruyère or Cheddar cheese.
* Add breadcrumbs or panko crumbs on top before baking.

4. Remove from heat; stir in half the Swiss cheese until melted. Add the cauliflower, stirring to coat. Pour into the baking dish and sprinkle with the remaining Swiss cheese and paprika. Bake immediately or cover and refrigerate to bake later.

5. Bake for 30 minutes, until hot and bubbly. If baking after being refrigerated, increase the baking time to 40 minutes.

Street Corn Salad

Serve this easy Street Corn Salad just once, and it will quickly become one of your favorite go-to side dishes for taco nights at home.

6 ears fresh corn

2 ½ tablespoons olive oil mayonnaise

½ teaspoon salt

½ teaspoon black pepper

½ teaspoon chili powder

¼ cup fresh lime juice

⅔ cup crumbled feta cheese

3 green onions, sliced

1. Preheat the oven to 400°F. Line a rimmed cookie sheet with aluminum foil, shiny-side up.

2. Place the corn on the baking sheet and brush all sides evenly with mayonnaise. Sprinkle with the salt, black pepper, and chili powder. Bake for 30 to 35 minutes, turning the corn every 10 minutes, until tender and slightly charred.

3. Remove the corn from the oven and cut the kernels off the cobs into a large bowl. Add the lime juice, feta cheese, and sliced green onions; toss gently. Season with more salt and black pepper (if desired). Chill until ready to serve.

MAKE-AHEAD
NUT-FREE
GLUTEN-FREE
VEGETARIAN

SERVES: **6**

Per Serving

Calories: 196; Total Fat: 8g; Saturated Fat: 3g; Carbohydrates: 29g; Fiber: 4g; Protein: 7g

Cranberry Broccoli Slaw

Crunchy and sweet, this quick slaw can be served immediately, but the flavors will meld more if allowed to chill for 30 minutes.

1 (12-ounce) package broccoli slaw mix

⅓ cup dried cranberries

¼ cup slivered almonds

⅓ cup olive-oil mayonnaise

2 tablespoons honey

1 tablespoon apple cider vinegar

½ teaspoon kosher salt

¼ teaspoon black pepper

1. In a large bowl, toss the broccoli slaw mix, cranberries, and almonds together.

2. In another bowl, stir together the mayonnaise, honey, apple cider vinegar, salt, and black pepper until smooth. Pour the mixture over the broccoli slaw and stir until coated. Refrigerate until ready to serve.

NO-COOK
GLUTEN-FREE
DAIRY-FREE
VEGETARIAN

SERVES: 8

Per Serving

Calories: 104; Total Fat: 5g;
Saturated Fat: 0g;
Carbohydrates: 15g;
Fiber: 2g; Protein: 2g

Flavor Swap:

* Make a broccoli salad by using one head of broccoli broken into small florets instead of broccoli slaw mix.

Watermelon Salad

This refreshing salad of bite-size watermelon cubes is tossed with a simple lime-honey dressing. For a fun serving idea, cut the watermelon into small, pie-shaped wedges and serve them on a plate drizzled with dressing and crumbled feta cheese.

4 cups cubed watermelon

1 teaspoon mint leaves, minced

Juice from 1 lime

1 tablespoon honey

⅓ cup crumbled feta cheese

1. In a large bowl, gently toss the watermelon with the mint leaves.

2. In a small bowl, stir together the lime juice and honey. Pour the mixture over the watermelon. Top with the feta cheese. Serve immediately.

NO-COOK
NUT-FREE
GLUTEN-FREE
SOY-FREE
VEGETARIAN

SERVES: **8**

Per Serving

Calories: 45; Total Fat: 1g;
Saturated Fat: 1g;
Carbohydrates: 9g;
Fiber: 1g; Protein: 1g

Tip:

* Leftover watermelon can get mushy or "mealy," so this dish is best served immediately. Store uncut watermelon in the bottom of the refrigerator to chill before slicing.

Tabbouleh

PREP TIME: 15 MINUTES

A vegan Lebanese salad, tabbouleh is traditionally made with bulgur wheat. However, in a pinch, you may substitute cooked couscous. Also, feel free to add more lemon or mint to suit your taste.

½ cup dry bulgur wheat

Water

1½ cups finely chopped parsley leaves (the curly kind, not Italian flat leaf)

½ cup chopped fresh mint leaves

2 medium-size tomatoes, diced

3 tablespoons extra-virgin olive oil

Juice from ½ large lemon (about 3 tablespoons)

1 teaspoon kosher salt

½ teaspoon freshly ground black pepper

1. In a small bowl, add the bulgur wheat and just enough cold water to cover it. Soak for about 15 minutes or until all the water is absorbed.

2. Combine the bulgur with the parsley, mint, and tomatoes. Toss gently with the olive oil and lemon juice. Season with the salt and black pepper, adding more or less to your taste.

NO-COOK
NUT-FREE
SOY-FREE
VEGAN

SERVES: 8

Per Serving

Calories: 88; Total Fat: 6g; Saturated Fat: 1g; Carbohydrates: 10g; Fiber: 3g; Protein: 2g

Tip:

* Remember to remove the parsley leaves and discard the stems before chopping them. Pulsing for a few seconds in a food processor works well for this task.

Roasted Brussels Sprouts with Pancetta and Pecans

PREP TIME: 5 MINUTES / COOK TIME: 25 MINUTES

Roasting Brussels sprouts brings out their nutty, savory flavor. When we add pancetta and pecans to this dish, you have a delicious match made in heaven.

1 pound Brussels sprouts

⅓ cup pancetta, diced

⅓ cup pecans, coarsely chopped

2 tablespoons extra-virgin olive oil

Kosher salt

Freshly ground black pepper

1. Preheat the oven to 425°F. Slice the Brussels sprouts in half and place on a rimmed baking sheet. If they have larger heads, cut them into 3 or 4 slices instead of halves.

2. Add the pancetta and pecans and drizzle with olive oil, tossing until evenly coated. Make sure most of the Brussel sprouts are cut-side down. Season with salt and pepper.

3. Bake for 25 to 30 minutes, or until tender and caramelized.

EASY CLASSIC
GLUTEN-FREE
DAIRY-FREE
SOY-FREE

SERVES: 4

Per Serving

Calories: 209; Total Fat: 17g;
Saturated Fat: 3g;
Carbohydrates: 12g;
Fiber: 5g; Protein: 7g

Orange-Kissed Carrots

A splash of citrus makes all the difference in these traditional honey-glazed carrots.

Water

1 pound baby carrots

½ teaspoon kosher salt, plus more for seasoning

2 tablespoons unsalted butter

2 tablespoons honey

Juice and zest from 1 orange

Freshly ground black pepper

1 teaspoon fresh thyme leaves, optional

1. Bring water to a boil over medium-high heat. Add the carrots and ½ teaspoon salt (*Note: If the water does not cover the carrots, add more and return to a boil*). Cook for 5 to 6 minutes, or until tender.

2. Drain off the water and return the pan to heat. Add the butter, honey, and orange juice. Continue cooking about 5 minutes, or until carrots are glazed and liquid is reduced.

3. To serve, season with salt and freshly ground black pepper and garnish with orange zest and fresh thyme leaves (if desired).

EASY CLASSIC
NUT-FREE
GLUTEN-FREE
SOY-FREE
VEGETARIAN

SERVES: **8**

Per Serving

Calories: 66; Total Fat: 3g;
Saturated Fat: 2g;
Carbohydrates: 10g;
Fiber: 2g; Protein: 1g

Sour Cream Mashed Potatoes

PREP TIME: 10 MINUTES / COOK TIME: 20 MINUTES

These potatoes have half the calories that the ones my mom used to make with heavy cream and a whole stick of butter! Even so, they're still quite delicious. The best part is that they make a tasty side dish for several dinner recipes in this book.

8 medium-size Yukon Gold potatoes, peeled and cut into cubes

Water

3 tablespoons unsalted butter

¼ cup low-fat milk

1½ teaspoon kosher salt

½ cup low-fat sour cream

1 tablespoon fresh chives, minced

1. Place the potatoes in a large pot and cover them with water. Bring to a boil over medium-high heat.

2. Reduce heat to medium and cook at a slow boil for 15 to 20 minutes, or until the potatoes are fork tender.

3. Remove from heat and drain. Add the butter, milk, and salt to the potatoes and whip with a hand-held mixer until most of the lumps are gone. You can also use a hand-held potato masher.

4. Stir in the sour cream and chives. Add salt (if needed). Serve immediately.

EASY CLASSIC
NUT-FREE
GLUTEN-FREE
SOY-FREE
VEGETARIAN

SERVES: **8**

Per Serving

Calories: 230; Total Fat: 6g;
Saturated Fat: 4g;
Carbohydrates: 40g;
Fiber: 3g; Protein: 5g

Substitution Tip:

* If you want to save even more calories, use low-sodium chicken broth in place of the milk.

Use the Leftovers:

* Make a hearty and filling Shepherd's Pie (see page 87) with leftover Sour Cream Mashed Potatoes and Sloppy Joes (see page 68).
* Make Hot Potato Cakes (see page 114).

Lemon-Basil Potato Salad

This yummy potato salad recipe is full of fresh lemon and basil flavor.

For the potato salad:

1 pound small Yukon gold potatoes, unpeeled and quartered

Water

1 cup coarsely chopped Perfectly Roasted Asparagus (see page 98)

¼ red onion, thinly sliced

For the vinaigrette:

¼ cup olive oil

¼ cup fresh lemon juice

1 tablespoon chopped fresh basil

1 tablespoon white wine vinegar

1 garlic clove, minced

1 teaspoon sugar

¼ teaspoon salt

¼ teaspoon freshly ground black pepper

REINVENTION
NUT-FREE
GLUTEN-FREE
VEGAN

SERVES: **6**

Per Serving

Calories: 137; Total Fat: 9g;
Saturated Fat: 1g;
Carbohydrates: 14g;
Fiber: 3g; Protein: 2g

1. Place the potatoes in a saucepan and cover with water.

2. Bring to a boil over high heat. Cover and reduce heat to medium-low. Cook for 15 to 20 minutes, until tender. Drain and rinse with cool water.

3. In a large bowl, add the potatoes, asparagus, and red onion.

4. To make the vinaigrette: Whisk together all the vinaigrette ingredients and pour over the vegetables. Toss gently. This dish may be served warm or chilled.

Caprese Pasta Salad

PREP TIME: 15 MINUTES

In the time it takes pasta to cook, you can have the rest of the ingredients chopped and prepped for this simple salad. Toss it all together and serve immediately, or, if you'd prefer it cold, chill it in the refrigerator and add Parmesan cheese and basil garnish just before serving.

2 cups dry pasta (bowtie or spiral)

1 large tomato, diced

½ pound (8 ounces) fresh mozzarella cheese, broken into chunks

½ cup Sundried Tomato Vinaigrette (see page 47)

Salt

Freshly ground black pepper

¼ cup freshly grated Parmesan cheese

¼ cup chopped fresh basil

1. Cook the pasta according to package directions; rinse with cold water and drain.

2. In a large bowl, add the pasta, tomato, and mozzarella cheese. Pour the vinaigrette on top and toss gently. Season with salt and freshly ground black pepper, to taste.

3. To serve, garnish with freshly grated Parmesan cheese and fresh basil.

REINVENTION
NUT-FREE
GLUTEN-FREE
VEGETARIAN

SERVES: **4**

Per Serving

Calories: 361; Total Fat: 24g;
Saturated Fat: 8g;
Carbohydrates: 25g;
Fiber: 2g; Protein: 12g

Hot Potato Cakes

PREP TIME: 10 MINUTES / COOK TIME: 10 MINUTES

Growing up, my mom never let leftovers go to waste. Potato cakes, however, were always my favorite. Most times, she would put yesterday's mashed potatoes in a pie plate, dot the top with butter, and heat it up in the oven until the top was golden and crusty. I've added green onions and a jalapeño pepper to Mom's original recipe to kick it up a notch.

2 cups chilled Sour Cream Mashed Potatoes (see page 111)

1 egg, slightly beaten

¼ cup all-purpose flour

¼ cup green onions, diced

½ jalapeño pepper, seeded and diced

1 teaspoon kosher salt

¼ teaspoon freshly ground black pepper

2 tablespoons canola oil

1. In a large bowl, mix the potatoes, egg, flour, green onions, jalapeño pepper, salt, and black pepper.

2. Heat the canola oil in a large skillet over medium-high heat. Working in batches, use a ¼-cup measure to scoop the potato mixture into the hot pan. Flatten each cake out to about ½-inch thickness.

3. Cook for about 3 minutes on each side, until golden brown. Serve immediately.

REINVENTION
NUT-FREE
GLUTEN-FREE
SOY-FREE
VEGETARIAN

SERVES: **6**

Per Serving

Calories: 158; Total Fat: 6g; Saturated Fat: 1g; Carbohydrates: 24g; Fiber: 3g; Protein: 4g

Warm Apple Baked Brie, page 120

CHAPTER SIX

Snacks

Are you a nibbler? I am. That's why I try to avoid stocking potato chips in our pantry—it takes all my will power to resist their salty crunch! To solve that problem, I like to make healthy snacks, like the Peanut Butter Oatmeal Energy Balls or Spicy Skillet Chickpeas found in this chapter. You'll also find dips—like Butternut Squash Hummus or Tzatziki Dip—that are great to serve with raw veggies. In addition to everyday snacks, I've included a few party appetizer recipes like Bruschetta, Warm Apple Baked Brie, and Mango Salsa that I hope you will enjoy.

Popcorn snack attack.

Let me give you a fair warning: I'll share any of my food with you, but don't even think about messing with my popcorn. Really. My affection for it is serious.

Long before we ever owned a popcorn maker or had microwave popcorn bags, I learned how to make popcorn the old-fashioned way by shaking a hot pan on top of the stove and listening for the kernels to pop, sizzle, and steam until the lid raised and the popcorn literally began to overflow. On Saturday nights, my sister and I would make a big batch of popcorn, divide it into bowls, pour on salt and melted butter, and settle in to watch the latest episodes of *The Love Boat* and *Charlie's Angels*. I was a happy girl when I had my own bowl of buttery popcorn.

One Halloween, my dad decided he wanted popcorn balls, a treat his grandmother used to make. He popped a huge tub of popcorn, salted it well, and mixed in molasses with a wooden spoon. I remember he buttered his hands, formed the mixture into balls as big as softballs, and wrapped each one in wax paper. Sweet, salty, crunchy—all my favorite attributes in one handheld treat—*and* we each had our own. No sharing. These days, instead of popcorn balls, making caramel corn with pecans and cashews is our fall indulgence.

My husband often teases that he'd lose an arm if he tried to sneak a bite from my popcorn bag when we're at the movies. Who could resist movie theater popcorn? Not me, so get your own bag! Just teasing . . . sort of.

I'm a big fan of plain buttered popcorn, white Cheddar popcorn, kettle corn, caramel corn, Moose Munch, and Cracker Jacks, so how could I include a snack chapter without at least one homemade popcorn recipe? The Savory Rosemary Parmesan Popcorn (see page 123) is seasoned with an herb-infused olive oil making it a lighter, deliciously satisfying snack. The recipe yields 12 cups of popcorn—plenty to share—but, if you're with me, grab your own bowl.

Tiki Snack Mix

PREP TIME: 5 MINUTES / COOK TIME: 20 MINUTES

Perfect for an outdoor summer party, this sweet and salty snack will keep guests migrating back to the bowl for handful after handful.

2½ cups lightly salted dry roasted peanuts

2 cups candied pineapple (or candied pineapple rings), cut into small pieces

2 tablespoons sesame seeds

1½ tablespoons soy sauce

1½ tablespoons honey

¼ teaspoon red cayenne pepper

Kosher salt

1. Preheat the oven to 350°F.

2. Combine the peanuts, candied pineapple, and sesame seeds on a rimmed baking sheet.

3. In a small bowl, stir together the soy sauce, honey, and red cayenne pepper and drizzle over the snack mix. Stir with a rubber spatula until the mix is evenly coated.

4. Bake for 20 minutes, stirring after 10 minutes. Remove from the oven and sprinkle with salt. Cool completely on a wire rack before removing from pan. Store tightly covered for 2 weeks.

ONE-POT
GLUTEN-FREE
VEGETARIAN

YIELDS **4½ CUPS**

Per Serving (½ cup)

Calories: 365, Total Fat: 21g;
Saturated Fat: 3g;
Carbohydrates: 38g;
Fiber: 4g; Protein: 10g

Tip:

★ Give the snack mix a stir occasionally as it cools to break it into chunks.

Warm Apple Baked Brie

PREP TIME: 5 MINUTES / COOK TIME: 10 MINUTES

This simply elegant snack or party appetizer is ready in just 15 minutes, and it's the ultimate crowd pleaser at any holiday gathering.

2 apples, cored and thinly sliced (see Tip)

1 (8-ounce) Brie cheese round

2 to 3 tablespoons molasses (or honey)

1 tablespoon brown sugar

¼ cup chopped walnuts

1 small baguette

1. Preheat the oven to 400°F.

2. Arrange the apples around the Brie on an oven-proof serving plate. Drizzle molasses over the apples and Brie, then sprinkle with brown sugar and walnuts.

3. Bake for about 10 minutes, or until the apples are just tender.

4. Slice the baguette for serving. If desired, heat the bread on another baking pan during the last 5 minutes of baking.

ONE-POT VEGETARIAN

SERVES: 6

Per Serving

Calories: 343; Total Fat: 14g; Saturated Fat: 7g; Carbohydrates: 42g; Fiber: 3g; Protein: 14g

Tip:

★ Gala apples work nicely in this recipe.

Spicy Skillet Chickpeas

PREP TIME: 5 MINUTES / COOK TIME: 5 MINUTES

Fresh lime juice adds just the right punch to this spicy, crunchy snack.

1 (15-ounce) can chickpeas (garbanzo beans)

1 tablespoon extra-virgin olive oil

1 teaspoon fresh lime juice

½ teaspoon smoked paprika

½ teaspoon cumin

½ teaspoon sea salt

¼ teaspoon freshly ground black pepper

2½ tablespoons canola oil

1. Rinse the chickpeas, drain well, and dry in a dish-towel. Place a second towel on top and gently roll to loosen skins, discarding as many as you can.

2. In a small bowl, mix together the olive oil, lime juice, smoked paprika, cumin, salt, and black pepper.

3. Heat the canola oil in a skillet over medium-high heat. Carefully add the chickpeas; cook and stir for 5 to 6 minutes until browned and crispy, being careful not to burn them.

4. Remove the chickpeas to a paper towel–lined bowl and wipe out any remaining oil from the skillet.

5. Return the chickpeas to the skillet, adding the olive oil and lime mixture. Cook and stir for 20 to 30 seconds until well coated. Remove to a serving bowl; cool for a few minutes before serving.

ONE-POT
NUT-FREE
GLUTEN-FREE
SOY-FREE
VEGAN

SERVES: **6**

Per Serving

Calories: 146; Total Fat: 9g; Saturated Fat: 1g; Carbohydrates: 14g; Fiber: 3g; Protein: 3g

Tip:

★ It's important to dry the chickpeas and remove the skins. They will get crisper more quickly when cooking.

Bruschetta

PREP TIME: 15 MINUTES / COOK TIME: 15 MINUTES

The secret to an amazing bruschetta is choosing beautifully ripe tomatoes. The redder the tomatoes, the better the flavor.

1 baguette

1 garlic clove, halved

3 tablespoons extra-virgin olive oil, divided

3 medium ripe red tomatoes

¼ cup finely chopped red onion

1 tablespoon traditional aged balsamic vinegar

Kosher salt

Freshly ground black pepper

1 tablespoon fresh basil leaves, cut into a *chiffonade* (see Tip)

MAKE-AHEAD
EASY CLASSIC
NUT-FREE
DAIRY-FREE
VEGETARIAN

SERVES: 6

Per Serving

Calories: 263; Total Fat: 8g;
Saturated Fat: 1g;
Carbohydrates: 40g;
Fiber: 2g; Protein: 8g

Tip:

★ Chiffonade is a slicing technique for cutting fresh leaves into a thin ribbon garnish. To cut a basil chiffonade, stack a few leaves on top of each other and roll them up tightly on the long side. Cut into very thin slices, then separate them into ribbons.

1. Preheat the oven to 350°F. Slice the baguette into ¼-inch slices and place the slices on a baking sheet. Rub the slices with the garlic clove and drizzle lightly with 2 tablespoons of olive oil. Toast them in the oven for 10 to 15 minutes, until golden brown. Remove and cool. Store in a sealed container until ready to use.

2. To make the bruschetta: Dice the tomatoes and place them in a shallow dish with the red onion. Drizzle with the remaining olive oil and balsamic vinegar. Season with salt and black pepper.

3. Allow the bruschetta to rest for 10 to 15 minutes for the flavors to meld. Garnish with basil and serve with baguette toasts.

Savory Rosemary Parmesan Popcorn

PREP TIME: 15 MINUTES / COOK TIME: 15 MINUTES

This is a wonderfully cheesy popcorn that is seasoned with herb-infused olive oil. You will become enamored of this dish as I have.

2 tablespoons extra-virgin olive oil

2 sprigs fresh rosemary, divided

½ teaspoon garlic salt

12 cups cooked popcorn (see Tip)

¼ cup Parmesan cheese

1. Heat the olive oil and 1 rosemary sprig in a small sauce pan over medium heat for 2 to 3 minutes, infusing the oil.

2. Remove the cooked rosemary sprig. Once it cools, mince the leaves. Stir back into the olive oil along with the garlic salt.

3. Place the popcorn in a large bowl and drizzle with the infused oil. Toss to coat.

4. Mince the remaining sprig of rosemary and sprinkle it over the popcorn with the Parmesan cheese. Toss gently and serve.

MAKE-AHEAD
NUT-FREE
SOY-FREE
VEGETARIAN

YIELDS **12 CUPS**

Per Serving (2 cups)

Calories: 118; Total Fat: 6g;
Saturated Fat: 1g;
Carbohydrates: 13g;
Fiber: 2g; Protein: 4g

Tip:

* To get the 12 cups of popcorn, use ½ cup kernels or a 3-serving microwave bag, not butter-flavored.

Peanut Butter Oatmeal Energy Balls

PREP TIME: 15 MINUTES / CHILL TIME: 30 MINUTES

Satisfy that cookie craving with these tasty no-bake energy balls made with whole grains.

1 cup old-fashioned oats

¼ cup peanut butter (smooth or chunky)

¼ cup mini chocolate chips

¼ cup honey

⅓ cup flax seeds

½ teaspoon vanilla extract

Pinch kosher salt

1. Using a wooden spoon or heavy spatula, stir together all the ingredients in a large bowl until coated. If the mixture seems too wet or sticky, add a few more oats. If the mixture seems too dry, add a bit more honey. Refrigerate for at least 30 minutes.

2. Remove the mixture from refrigerator and portion out the balls using a 1-ounce scoop. Using your palms and fingers, press each portion into a small ball. Note: do not "roll" the mixture into balls; instead, shape the mixture lightly using the pressure of your fingers.

3. Store in an airtight container.

Flavor Swaps:

* Instead of mini chocolate chips, try mini M&Ms for a more colorful snack.
* Try chia seeds or sunflower kernels instead of flax seeds, or use a mixture of seeds.

MAKE-AHEAD

NO-COOK

VEGETARIAN

YIELDS **16 BALLS**

Per Serving (1 ball)

Calories: 89; Total Fat: 4g;
Saturated Fat: 1g;
Carbohydrates: 12g;
Fiber: 2g; Protein: 2g

Tips:

* The secret to this recipe is making sure you get a good balance of dry ingredients to the peanut butter and honey, which will bind it all together.
* It's also important to let the mixture chill for at least 30 minutes before forming it into balls.

Creamy Bean Dip

PREP TIME: 5 MINUTES

To make this dip genuinely vegetarian, choose canned pinto beans that have not been seasoned with pork. Vegetarian or carnivore, this dip will satisfy all.

1 (15-ounce) can pinto beans

1 (4-ounce) can green chiles

1 small tomato, chopped

1½ cups shredded Monterey Jack cheese

¼ cup light sour cream

2 teaspoons chili powder

½ teaspoon kosher salt

¼ teaspoon cumin

1. Place the pinto beans, green chiles, and tomato in a food processor and blend until smooth. Add the Monterey Jack cheese, sour cream, chili powder, salt, and cumin. Blend until creamy and thick. (If you like it milder, only use 1 teaspoon of chili powder.)

2. Garnish with additional diced tomato, green onions, or cilantro (if desired). Serve with tortilla chips or raw veggie sticks. Refrigerate leftovers for up to a week.

NO-COOK
NUT-FREE
VEGETARIAN

SERVES: **8**

Per Serving

Calories: 188; Total Fat: 9g;
Saturated Fat: 5g;
Carbohydrates: 19g;
Fiber: 7g; Protein: 10g

Flavor Swap:

* For a spicier dip, use a fresh jalapeño pepper in place of the canned green chiles.

Use the Leftovers:

* Use this recipe to make my Bean Dip Roll-Ups (see page 133).

Tip:

* This dip can be served warm or cold. To heat, top with more shredded Monterey Jack cheese and warm in a 350° oven until the cheese is melted and bubbly.

GORP Trail Mix

GORP, or "good old raisins and peanuts," is a term commonly used for trail mix by hikers. This snack is easy to pack and eat on the run whether you're a hiker or not.

1 cup toasted oat cereal (like Cheerios)

1 cup salted peanuts

1 cup golden raisins

1 cup M&M's

1 cup dried banana chips

Mix all the ingredients together in a large bowl. Store in an airtight container or portion out into individual resealable plastic bags for easy snacking.

NO-COOK
VEGETARIAN

YIELDS 5 CUPS

Per Serving (½ cup)

Calories: 194; Total Fat: 11g; Saturated Fat: 4g; Carbohydrates: 23g; Fiber: 3g; Protein: 5g

Flavor Swaps:

* Use granola or a sweetened cereal like Honey Nut Cheerios or Frosted Flakes.
* Mix and match dried fruits or nuts to suit your tastes. Some options include dried apple chips, dried mango or apricot, almonds, sunflower seeds, or spicy corn nuts.

Tzatziki Dip and Homemade Pita Chips

PREP TIME: 10 MINUTES

With fresh mint and cool cucumber, Tzatziki Dip is usually served alongside lamb or chicken gyros. My family, however, enjoys eating this dip with homemade pita chips.

For the dip:
1 English cucumber

2 green onions, minced

2 cups plain Greek yogurt

4 tablespoons chopped fresh mint leaves

1 teaspoon kosher salt

For the homemade pita chips:
6 pita bread rounds

2 tablespoons extra-virgin olive oil

1 teaspoon dried oregano

EASY CLASSIC
NUT-FREE
SOY-FREE
VEGETARIAN

YIELDS **2 CUPS**

Per Serving (½ cup)

Calories: 268; Total Fat: 10g;
Saturated Fat: 2g;
Carbohydrates: 32g;
Fiber: 4g; Protein: 17g

To make the dip:
1. Slice the cucumber in half longways. Scoop out the seeds with a small spoon and discard. Grate the cucumber with a box grater; squeeze in a paper towel to remove moisture.

2. Add the cucumber and green onion to the yogurt along with the mint and salt. Stir to combine. Serve immediately with pita chips or raw veggies.

To make the pita chips:
1. Preheat the oven to 400° F.

2. Cut each pita into 8 wedges. Arrange the wedges on a large baking sheet. Brush with olive oil. Toss and spread evenly. Sprinkle with the oregano and bake for 8 to 12 minutes, until toasted and golden.

Jalapeño Pimento Cheese

PREP TIME: 15 MINUTES

You'll likely find some sort of pimento cheese sandwiches at a casual Southern party—the inspiration for this classic dish. For snacking, serve it on crackers or with vegetable sticks.

1 (8-ounce) package low-fat cream cheese, softened

1 (8-ounce) sharp white cheddar cheese, shredded

1 jalapeño pepper, seeds removed and diced

1 (2-ounce) jar diced pimento (do not drain)

2 tablespoons minced white onion

¼ teaspoon garlic powder

¼ teaspoon kosher salt

⅛ teaspoon red cayenne pepper

1. Using a handheld mixer, beat the cream cheese until smooth in a large bowl. Add the remaining ingredients and mix well.

2. Serve with crackers or raw veggies.

Use the Leftovers:

★ Use this recipe to make my Ham and Cheese Pinwheels (see page 131).

NO-COOK
EASY CLASSIC
NUT-FREE
GLUTEN-FREE
VEGETARIAN

SERVES: **8 TO 10**

Per Serving

Calories: 186; Total Fat: 16g;
Saturated Fat: 6g;
Carbohydrates: 4g;
Fiber: 1g; Protein: 10g

Tips:

★ If the cheese spread is too thick, add one or two tablespoons of plain Greek yogurt, low-fat mayonnaise, or sour cream.

★ It's not entirely necessary, but some like to roast or sauté the onions and jalapeños before mixing into their pimento cheese to give it a smokier flavor.

Charcuterie with Whipped Honey Ricotta

PREP TIME: 10 MINUTES

Pick up your favorite Italian cured meat, like prosciutto or Genoa salami, and combine it with juicy pears on top of a sliced baguette smeared with honey-sweetened whipped ricotta cheese. Easy enough for a quick snack and elegant enough to serve guests.

1 cup whole-milk ricotta

½ teaspoon lemon juice

½ tablespoon extra-virgin olive oil

Sea salt

2 tablespoons honey

Sliced pears (or apples)

Sliced Italian-cured meat (Genoa salami or prosciutto)

1 small baguette, sliced

1. In a small bowl, whisk together the ricotta, lemon juice, olive oil, and a sprinkle of salt. Add the honey and stir, adjusting the amount of honey to your taste.

2. Serve with sliced pears, Italian-cured meat, and your choice of crackers, thin breadsticks, or a sliced baguette.

NO-COOK
EASY CLASSIC
NUT-FREE

YIELDS **1 CUP**

Per Serving

Calories: 387; Total Fat: 20g; Saturated Fat: 9g; Carbohydrates: 37g; Fiber: 2g; Protein: 17g

Tips:

* To build a balanced cheese board, choose three cheeses—one hard aged, one soft/semi-soft or cheese spread, and one blue.
* Choose something salty or briny (e.g., salami or prosciutto) or olives or nuts.
* Add something sweet (e.g., honey or jam) to help balance the cheese.
* Add fresh or dried fruit.

Mango Salsa

This easy salsa uses all fresh ingredients. This salsa is perfect on its own as sweet and spicy dip or paired with my Baja Fish Tacos (see page 91).

2 just-ripe mangoes, peeled and diced (see Tip)

1 red bell pepper, seeded and diced

½ small red onion, finely chopped

1 jalapeño pepper, seeded and diced

Juice from 1 small lime (about 2 tablespoons)

Sea salt

1. Add the diced mango, bell pepper, onion, and jalapeño pepper to a bowl. Squeeze in the lime juice and stir gently.

2. Season with salt to taste. Serve immediately with tortilla chips or chill in the refrigerator for later.

Flavor Swap:

★ Instead of mango, try this recipe with fresh pineapple. You may also toss in a handful of chopped fresh cilantro.

NO-COOK
EASY CLASSIC
NUT-FREE
GLUTEN-FREE
SOY-FREE
VEGAN

YIELDS 1½ CUPS

Per Serving (¼ cup)

Calories: 80; Total Fat: 1g;
Saturated Fat: 0g;
Carbohydrates: 20g;
Fiber: 2g; Protein: 1g

Tip:

★ To dice a mango, slice off each side just past the seed. Take each piece and make slices in the flesh without breaking the skin. Scoop out the mango slices with a large spoon, then dice them into cubes.

Ham and Cheese Pinwheels

PREP TIME: 5 MINUTES

These pinwheels—secured with colorful toothpicks and placed on a platter—are a quick and fun party appetizer.

½ cup Jalapeño Pimento Cheese (see page 128)

4 slices deli ham

4 whole green onions

1. Divide and spread the cheese on to the ham slices. Top each piece with a whole green onion stalk and roll up tightly from the short side.

2. Slice each roll-up into 4 pinwheels and secure it closed with a toothpick. Serve them immediately or chill in the refrigerator for later.

NO-COOK
REINVENTION
NUT-FREE

SERVES: **4**

Per Serving

Calories: 81; Total Fat: 5g; Saturated Fat: 1g; Carbohydrates: 3g; Fiber: 1g; Protein: 6g

Flavor Swap:

* Try wrapping a dill pickle spear or pickled okra inside these pinwheels for a different flavor.

Butternut Squash Hummus

PREP TIME: 10 MINUTES / COOK TIME: 15 MINUTES

This is my favorite hummus for the fall season because of the hint of ground cinnamon.

1 (15-ounce) can chickpeas, drained

1½ cups roasted butternut squash (see page 101)

2 tablespoons tahini

½ cup plain Greek yogurt

2 tablespoons cold water

3 tablespoons extra-virgin olive oil, divided

1 teaspoon sea salt

1 teaspoon ground cinnamon, plus extra for garnish

1. In a small saucepan, add the chickpeas and cover them with water. Bring to a boil over medium heat; reduce heat and continue cooking for about 20 minutes, or until the chickpeas are soft.

2. Drain the chickpeas and place them in a food processor with the squash, tahini, Greek yogurt, water, and 2 tablespoons of olive oil. Blend until smooth. If too thick, add more olive oil or water.

3. Add the salt and cinnamon and blend again until well combined.

4. Serve in a shallow bowl drizzled with the remaining olive oil and a sprinkle of cinnamon.

REINVENTION
NUT-FREE
GLUTEN-FREE
VEGETARIAN

YIELDS **2 CUPS**

Per Serving (¼ cup)

Calories: 142; Total Fat: 8g;
Saturated Fat: 1g;
Carbohydrates: 14g;
Fiber: 3g; Protein: 5g

Bean Dip Roll-Ups

Sort of like a taquito, these Bean Dip Roll-Ups should be baked until they are warm and toasty. Be sure to use your favorite salsa as a dipping sauce.

8 tablespoons Creamy Bean Dip (see page 125)

4 small flour tortillas

½ cup shredded Cheddar cheese

½ cup tomatoes, diced

¼ cup green onions, diced

1 teaspoon canola oil

1. Preheat the oven to 400°F. Line a baking sheet with aluminum foil.

2. Spread 2 tablespoons of Creamy Bean Dip on each flour tortilla. Top with the Cheddar cheese, tomato, and green onion. Roll up and place the roll-ups seam-side down on the baking sheet.

3. Brush the roll-ups with canola oil. Bake for 10 minutes, until warm and toasty. Serve with your favorite salsa (if desired).

REINVENTION
NUT-FREE
SOY-FREE
VEGETARIAN

SERVES: **4**

Per Serving

Calories: 220; Total Fat: 12g;
Saturated Fat: 6g;
Carbohydrates: 21g;
Fiber: 6g; Protein: 10g

Blackberry Cobbler, page 141

CHAPTER SEVEN

Dessert

Growing up in the South, I was taught that hospitality meant offering a freshly brewed cup of coffee and dessert to anyone who dropped in for a visit. It didn't matter if it was a slice of pound cake, my grandmother's cobbler, homemade brownies, or, on special occasions, homemade ice cream. What mattered was the inevitable smiles and laughter that ensued. I hope you enjoy sharing these sweet treats with your family and friends, as well.

Desserts as a love language.

Maybe you've experienced firsthand the special love language that starts in a cook's heart—especially the unspoken language that pulses through someone who makes desserts as they mix, roll, and bake a special treat to share. Maybe it was your aunt's Italian cream cake at the annual family reunion, or a surprise box of your mom's homemade cookies delivered to your dorm room. It could even have been the simple fruit crisp the host shared at last weekend's dinner party. Whatever it was, it probably left you with a smile on your face, licking your lips, and overall just feeling good.

An occasional sweet indulgence is good for the soul. Even dietitians say desserts should not be off limits.[4] As a certified chocoholic, that's certainly music to my ears. We hear a lot of talk about how sharing a meal is not only beneficial for feeding our bodies, but is a wonderful opportunity to connect, build community, and de-stress after a busy day. All that is true, of course, but let's not forget the importance of enjoying dessert once in a while as well.

When it came to desserts, the loving cooks in my family each had their own specialty. My dear Aunt Ruth gifted our family with a fresh 12-layer apple stack cake every Christmas. At family reunions, my cousins would rush to snag a piece of Aunt Cloteal's old-fashioned custard meringue pies before going through the main food line—in fear there wouldn't be any left if they didn't get to it first! My husband's Granny made the best chocolate chip cookies; our family thought she had a secret recipe, but we were all surprised to learn it was Nestlé's Toll House recipe. Yet somehow, our Toll House cookies never tasted as good as Granny's—it must have been the *love* she put into baking and sharing those cookies with her grandchildren.

As you peruse the desserts in this chapter, please keep these things in mind:

* Live a little—desserts are meant to be enjoyed.
* You should not feel guilt or regret after eating dessert.

---

[4] Rachel Goodman, "Why Desserts Shouldn't Be Off Limits," *Rachel Good Nutrition* (blog), April 14, 2017.

* Eating chocolate cake is okay, but sometimes include health-conscious desserts like my Balsamic Strawberry Parfaits (see page 158).
* Practice moderation, of course, but a healthy lifestyle always has room for a sweet treat.

Like the cooks in my own family, you may already have a dessert specialty. If not, then I encourage you to have fun discovering your own sweet love language and sharing it happily with those you love.

Chocolate Pudding Cake

PREP TIME: 5 MINUTES / COOK TIME: 45 MINUTES

This rich and simple cake is equally delicious served warm or cold with a scoop of vanilla ice cream. Resist the urge to stir the water into the batter during the last step. As it bakes, it will be absorbed, creating a yummy and gooey chocolate sauce.

Cooking spray

1 cup self-rising flour

1⅓ cups sugar, divided

6 tablespoons cocoa, divided

½ cup milk

¼ cup canola oil

1 teaspoon vanilla extract

1 cup boiling water

1. Preheat the oven to 350°F. Lightly coat the bottom of a 9-by-9-inch square baking pan with cooking spray.

2. Combine the flour with ⅔ cup sugar and 4 tablespoons cocoa. Add the milk, canola oil, and vanilla extract, stirring until well blended. Spread into the baking pan.

3. Combine the remaining sugar and cocoa and sprinkle it evenly over the batter.

4. Carefully pour the boiling water evenly over top of the sugar mixture in pan. DO NOT stir. Bake for 45 minutes. Serve warm or cold with ice cream (if desired).

ONE-POT
NUT-FREE
VEGETARIAN

SERVES: **6**

Per Serving

Calories: 356; Total Fat: 11g; Saturated Fat: 1g; Carbohydrates: 66g; Fiber: 2g; Protein: 4g

Flavor Swap:

* If you like nuts, feel free to add a few chopped pecans or walnuts to the batter before baking.

Individual Seasonal Fruit Crisps

This recipe is awesome. Choose your favorite in-season fruit or berries, top them with a buttery oat crumble, then bake and serve these crisps in individual ramekins to your favorite people (including yourself).

2½ tablespoons butter, softened, plus more to grease ramekins

2 cups fresh fruit, peeled and sliced or diced

¼ cup coconut sugar, plus 4 teaspoons to sweeten fruit, optional

¼ cup all-purpose flour

⅓ cup old-fashioned rolled oats

1. Preheat the oven to 375°F. Lightly coat the inside of 4 (6-ounce) ramekins with butter and place on a foil-lined baking sheet.

2. Add ½ cup of the fruit to each ramekin and sprinkle with 1 teaspoon water. Add a teaspoon of coconut sugar (if desired).

3. To make the crumble: Combine ¼ cup coconut sugar, flour, old-fashioned rolled oats, and butter. Evenly divide and sprinkle on top of fruit.

4. Bake for 25 to 30 minutes, or until the fruit is soft and the crumble is golden.

ONE-POT
NUT-FREE
VEGETARIAN

SERVES: **4**

Per Serving

Calories: 199; Total Fat: 8g; Saturated Fat: 5g; Carbohydrates: 32g; Fiber: 2g; Protein: 3g

Tips:

★ Always use fruit that is in season for the best results.

★ Most fruit will not need to be sweetened, but if the fruit or berries you choose seem tart, sprinkle them with a teaspoon of sugar before topping with the crumble.

Flavor Suggestions:

★ Consider incorporating fruit like cherries, berries, peaches, or apples in your fruit crisps.

Fudgy One-Bowl Brownies

PREP TIME: 5 MINUTES / COOK TIME: 30 MINUTES

These rich and fudgy dark chocolate brownies will satisfy any chocoholic's craving.

Cooking spray

4 squares (2 ounces) unsweetened baking
   chocolate, melted

8 tablespoons unsalted butter, melted

1 cup sugar

2 eggs

1 teaspoon vanilla extract

⅔ cup all-purpose flour

¼ teaspoon baking powder

¼ teaspoon salt

1. Preheat the oven to 350°F. Line a 9-by-9-inch
   square baking pan with aluminum foil overlapping
   the sides. Lightly coat with cooking spray.

2. Combine the chocolate and butter until smooth.
   Stir in the sugar, then add the eggs and vanilla
   extract. Beat well.

3. Sift the flour, baking powder, and salt directly into
   bowl. Stir until completely incorporated. Spread
   the batter into the baking dish.

4. Bake for 28 to 30 minutes, until the brownies
   begin to pull away from the sides of the pan. Cool
   completely before cutting into squares.

ONE-POT
NUT-FREE
VEGETARIAN

YIELDS
16 BROWNIES

Per Serving (1 brownie)
Calories: 196; Total Fat: 14g;
Saturated Fat: 8g;
Carbohydrates: 21g;
Fiber: 3g; Protein: 3g

Tips:
* Using a plastic knife to
  cut brownies gives a
  cleaner slice and helps
  keep crumbling to
  a minimum.
* Serve warm brownies
  with a scoop of vanilla
  ice cream; drizzle
  them with my Boozy
  Chocolate Sauce
  (see page 142) for
  extra decadence.

Blackberry Cobbler

PREP TIME: 15 MINUTES / COOK TIME: 45 MINUTES

This is my grandmother's fresh berry cobbler recipe, and is best served hot from the oven with a scoop of vanilla ice cream.

8 tablespoons unsalted butter

1 cup all-purpose flour

2 teaspoons baking powder

½ teaspoon kosher salt

1¼ cups sugar, divided

1 cup milk

1 quart fresh blackberries

1. Preheat the oven to 350°F. Melt the butter in a glass baking dish in the oven.

2. Stir together the flour, baking powder, and salt. Whisk in 1 cup sugar and milk until smooth.

3. Remove the dish from the oven and pour the batter on top of the melted butter—DO NOT stir. Evenly spoon the blackberries on top and sprinkle with the remaining ¼ cup sugar.

4. Bake for about 45 minutes, or until cobbler is golden and bubbly. Serve immediately with vanilla ice cream or whipped cream (if desired).

ONE-POT
NUT-FREE
VEGETARIAN

SERVES: 8

Per Serving

Calories: 322; Total Fat: 13g; Saturated Fat: 8g; Carbohydrates: 52g; Fiber: 4g; Protein: 4g

Flavor Swap:

★ This easy cobbler can be made with any type of fresh fruit or berries, like blueberries or peaches.

Boozy Chocolate Sauce

PREP TIME: 5 MINUTES / COOK TIME: 10 MINUTES / COOL TIME: 30 MINUTES

For an easy, decadent dessert, serve my Boozy Chocolate Sauce drizzled over a scoop of vanilla ice cream on top of a fresh peach half.

1 cup water

¼ cup sugar

⅓ cup white syrup (or blue agave nectar)

1 cup semisweet chocolate chips

¼ cup bourbon (or dark rum)

1. Bring the water, sugar, and white syrup to a boil over medium-high heat. Reduce heat to low and simmer for 10 minutes.

2. Remove from heat and stir in the semisweet chocolate chips and bourbon until melted. The sauce will be thin and will thicken when chilled.

3. Cool completely and store in the refrigerator for up to 2 weeks.

MAKE-AHEAD
NUT-FREE
GLUTEN-FREE
DAIRY-FREE
VEGETARIAN

YIELDS 1¾ CUPS

Per Serving (¼ cup)

Calories: 279; Total Fat: 9g;
Saturated Fat: 6g;
Carbohydrates: 43g;
Fiber: 0g; Protein: 2g

Flavor Swaps:

★ To use bittersweet baking chocolate in place of the chocolate chips, chop finely and increase the sugar to ⅓ cup.

Use the Leftovers:

★ Use this recipe with my Chocolate Bread Pudding (see page 159).

★ Serve drizzled over vanilla ice cream with Fudgy One-Bowl Brownies (see page 140).

No-Fail Pie Crust

PREP TIME: 10 MINUTES / CHILL TIME: 30 MINUTES

I never thought I could make my own pie crust until I tried this recipe. It really is easy to put together and makes for a delightfully flaky crust.

1¼ cups all-purpose flour

¼ teaspoon salt

½ teaspoon sugar

7 tablespoons cold butter, cut into cubes

5 tablespoons ice water, plus more if needed

1. Place the flour, salt, and sugar into a food processor and pulse a few times until blended.

2. Sprinkle the butter on top and pulse just until it is slightly broken into the flour, but still in visible pieces.

3. Sprinkle the ice water over the mixture and process just until the mixture starts to come together.

4. Dump the dough into a gallon-size zip-top plastic bag and press into a flat disk.

5. Refrigerate for 30 minutes or up to 1 day. You could freeze it for up to 1 month. When ready to make a pie, roll the dough out on a lightly floured piece of parchment paper.

MAKE-AHEAD
NO-COOK
NUT-FREE
VEGETARIAN

YIELDS **1 (9-INCH) PIE CRUST**

Per Serving (⅛ piece)

Calories: 161; Total Fat: 10g; Saturated Fat: 6g; Carbohydrates: 15g; Fiber: 1g; Protein: 2g

Tip:

* Set the chilled pie dough out for 10 to 15 minutes to make rolling into shape easier.

Use the Leftovers:

* Use this pie crust in my Rustic Apple Tart (see page 156).

Frozen Sugar Cookie Dough

PREP TIME: 15 MINUTES / CHILL TIME: 1 HOUR / COOK TIME: 15 MINUTES

Soft and not overly sweet, this versatile recipe is a fabulous match for your family's collection of cookie cutters. Sprinkle them with colorful decorating sugar or turbinado sugar before baking, or frost the baked cookies with a powdered sugar glaze. In a pinch, this recipe can also be used for a pie crust or cobbler topping.

3 cups all-purpose flour

2 teaspoons baking powder

1 teaspoon baking soda

¼ teaspoon salt

½ teaspoon nutmeg

½ cup butter, at room temperature

1 cup sugar

½ teaspoon vanilla extract

1 egg

¼ cup milk

1. Sift the flour, baking powder, baking soda, salt, and nutmeg into a bowl.

2. Using a stand mixer with a paddle, cream the butter, sugar, and vanilla extract until light and fluffy. Add the egg and milk and mix until incorporated. Slowly add the flour mixture on low speed and mix until the dough pulls away from bowl.

3. Divide the dough onto 2 sheets of plastic wrap. Fold the wrap over the dough, wrap tightly, and form a disc. Refrigerate for 1 hour.

4. To freeze, place the wrapped discs in a zip-top freezer bag *after* they have been chilled. Write the date and baking directions on the bag and freeze for up to 3 months.

MAKE-AHEAD
NUT-FREE
VEGETARIAN

YIELDS **4 TO 5 DOZEN COOKIES**

Per Serving (1 cookie)

Calories: 63; Total Fat: 2g; Saturated Fat: 1g; Carbohydrates: 10g; Fiber: 0g; Protein: 1g

Use the Leftovers:

* Use Frozen Sugar Cookie Dough to make Fruit Pizza (see page 157).

5. To bake immediately, roll the dough to ⅛-inch thickness on a floured surface and cut out with cookie cutters. Place on a baking sheet and sprinkle with decorating sugar.

6. To bake from frozen, thaw the dough overnight in the refrigerator first, then roll out and bake as directed below.

7. Bake the cookies at 350°F for 8 to 10 minutes, or until slightly golden around edges. Transfer to a wire rack to cool.

No-Churn Blueberry Ice Cream

PREP TIME: 15 MINUTES / FREEZE TIME: 6 HOURS

This recipe is perfect for making homemade ice cream without any extra equipment. Fold fresh blueberries into a creamy mix, pour into a loaf pan, and pop in your freezer until firm.

1 cup fresh blueberries

¼ cup sugar

1 teaspoon fresh lemon juice

2 cups heavy whipping cream, very cold

1 (14-ounce) can sweetened condensed milk

1 teaspoon vanilla extract

MAKE-AHEAD
NUT-FREE
GLUTEN-FREE
VEGETARIAN

SERVES: **12**

Per Serving

Calories: 291; Total Fat: 18g;
Saturated Fat: 11g;
Carbohydrates: 30g;
Fiber: 0g; Protein: 4g

Tip:

★ Let your bowl and beaters chill in the fridge for 30 minutes before whipping heavy cream, and you'll get stiff peaks much quicker.

1. Bring the blueberries, sugar, and lemon juice to a boil over medium-high heat. Reduce heat to low and gently boil for 5 to 10 minutes. Remove from the heat and cool completely.

2. Pour the heavy whipping cream into a cold bowl. Whip the cream with an electric mixer until stiff peaks form.

3. Pour the sweetened condensed milk into a large bowl and gently fold in the whipped cream and vanilla extract. Add the cooled blueberry mixture and stir until just combined.

4. Pour the ice cream into a loaf pan and cover the top with wax paper. Freeze for at least 6 hours (or overnight) until firm. This recipe will keep well for up to two weeks.

Strawberries and Cream Ice Box Cake

Layers of fresh strawberries, sweetened whipped cream, and graham crackers make this ice box cake so good, you won't believe how easy it is to make.

1 pound strawberries

2 cups heavy whipping cream

½ cup powdered sugar

1 teaspoon vanilla extract

1½ packs graham crackers

1. Hull and slice the strawberries, trying to keep the slices somewhat uniform in thickness.

2. Using an electric mixer with a wire whip attachment, beat the heavy whipping cream in a chilled mixing bowl until stiff peaks form. Add the powdered sugar and vanilla extract. Continue whipping until combined.

3. Spread just enough whipped cream to cover the bottom of a 9-by-9-inch square cake pan. Top with a layer of graham crackers, breaking them into pieces if needed to cover the entire surface, then add half the whipped cream and half the strawberries. Repeat layers, ending with strawberries on top.

4. Cover the cake with plastic wrap and refrigerate overnight. Cut into squares and serve.

NO-COOK
NUT-FREE
VEGETARIAN

SERVES: 9

Per Serving

Calories: 356; Total Fat: 23g;
Saturated Fat: 12g;
Carbohydrates: 37g;
Fiber: 2g; Protein: 3g

Tip:

* The ice box cake will be easier to serve if you pop it in the freezer for 30 minutes before cutting it into squares.

Chocolate-Peanut Butter Mousse

Get ready to layer two flavors of mousse, top them with a creamy chocolate ganache, and enjoy a rich and scrumptious little dessert.

1 pint heavy whipping cream, divided

1 cup semisweet chocolate chips

1 (8-ounce) package low-fat cream cheese, softened

1 cup creamy peanut butter

1 teaspoon vanilla extract

1 cup powdered sugar

NO-COOK
GLUTEN-FREE
VEGETARIAN

SERVES: 8

Per Serving

Calories: 656; Total Fat: 52g;
Saturated Fat: 25g;
Carbohydrates: 43g;
Fiber: 3g; Protein: 11g

Tip:

★ Cute little 5-ounce
glass jars hold the
perfect portion-size for
this mousse recipe.

1. Heat 1 cup of the heavy whipping cream for 60 seconds at 50 percent power in the micro-wave. Pour heated cream over the semisweet chocolate chips in a small bowl. Let chips melt without stirring.

2. Using an electric mixer with a wire whip attach-ment, beat the remaining heavy whipping cream in a chilled mixing bowl until stiff peaks form; refrigerate until ready to use.

3. Beat the cream cheese until smooth. Add the peanut butter, vanilla extract, and powdered sugar, and mix for 1 to 2 minutes, until fluffy. Transfer half of the mousse mixture to a separate bowl and set aside.

4. Gently stir the chocolate chips and cream until you have a smooth ganache. Pour ½ cup ganache into one of the mousse mixtures; beat until creamy.

5. Halve the whipped cream and gently fold it into each mixture—now you have one bowl of peanut butter mousse and one bowl of chocolate-peanut butter mousse.

6. Evenly layer the mousse into 8 small dessert bowls, with chocolate mousse on the bottom and chocolate–peanut butter mousse on top. Spoon a tablespoon of the remaining ganache over each serving. Chill for 30 minutes before serving.

Pineapple Fizz Slush

PREP TIME: 5 MINUTES

Cool and refreshing, experiment making this fruity drink with other tropical fruits.

1 pint vanilla (or coconut) ice cream

½ cup pineapple chunks

¼ cup coconut milk (or almond milk)

Ice

1 cup ginger ale

1. Place the ice cream, pineapple chunks, and coconut milk in a blender and blend at medium speed for 20 to 30 seconds until smooth.

2. Add about ½ cup ice to each glass. Pour mixture over the ice and top off with ginger ale. Garnish with a fresh pineapple slice (if desired).

NO-COOK
NUT-FREE
GLUTEN-FREE
VEGETARIAN

SERVES: **4**

Per Serving

Calories: 199; Total Fat: 12g;
Saturated Fat: 9g;
Carbohydrates: 21g;
Fiber: 1g; Protein: 2g

Crispy Coconut Balls

PREP TIME: 10 MINUTES / FREEZE TIME: 6 HOURS

My grandmother always made a batch of Crispy Coconut Balls every Christmas, but they're a yummy treat any time of year.

2 cups powdered sugar, divided

1 cup peanut butter

1 cup Rice Krispies cereal

Boiled water

1 cup shredded coconut

1. Cream together 1 cup of the powdered sugar with the peanut butter. Stir in the cereal and form into 1½-inch balls (or whatever size you prefer).

2. Make a paste: Place the remaining cup of the powdered sugar in a small bowl. Stir in the boiled water a little at a time until the sugar is smooth and the consistency of glue. If it gets too thin, add more powdered sugar.

3. Roll the balls in the powdered sugar paste, then roll them in the shredded coconut until coated completely. Place on a wax paper-lined tray until dry, then store in an airtight container for up to 2 weeks.

Tip:

✴ For the holidays, my grandmother would tint shredded coconut with red or green food coloring. To add the tint, place the shredded coconut in a resealable plastic bag with a few drops of food coloring, then seal and shake.

NO-COOK
DAIRY-FREE
VEGETARIAN

YIELDS
2 DOZEN BALLS

Per Serving (1 ball)

Calories: 119; Total Fat: 7g; Saturated Fat: 2g; Carbohydrates: 14g; Fiber: 1g; Protein: 3g

Flavor Swap:

✴ Make Crispy Chocolate Balls by dipping the balls in chocolate ganache instead of the powdered sugar paste and coconut. To make the ganache, place ½ cup chocolate chips in a small glass bowl. Heat the cream in the microwave for 20 to 30 seconds until hot—but not boiling—then pour it over the chocolate. Let it sit for 5 minutes, then stir until smooth.

Banana Pudding

Be careful you don't lick the spoon too many times while making the pudding for this recipe, or you may not have enough to finish the dish—this dessert is that yummy!

1 cup mascarpone cheese

1 cup heavy whipping cream

½ cup powdered sugar

½ teaspoon vanilla extract

¼ teaspoon salt

1 (11-ounce) box Nilla wafers

2 bananas, sliced

1. To make the pudding: Using an electric mixer with a wire whip attachment in a chilled mixing bowl, thoroughly whip the mascarpone cheese. Add the heavy whipping cream and continue whipping until thickened. Gradually add the powdered sugar, vanilla extract, and salt.

2. Line bottom of an 11-by-7-inch dish with Nilla wafers. Top with the sliced bananas and cover with the pudding. Crumble a few Nilla wafers over the top. Serve immediately or cover with plastic wrap and chill.

EASY CLASSIC NUT-FREE VEGETARIAN

SERVES: 6

Per Serving

Calories: 494; Total Fat: 31g; Saturated Fat: 15g; Carbohydrates: 53g; Fiber: 1g; Protein: 4g

Flavor Swap:

* To make a strawberry trifle, follow the directions for the pudding and pour it over lady fingers and strawberries instead of Nilla wafers and bananas.

Lemon Bars

PREP TIME: 15 MINUTES / COOK TIME: 35 MINUTES

Sweet and tart, these lemon bars are baked on top of a simple shortbread crust.

For the crust:

8 tablespoons cold butter, cut in small pieces

2 cups all-purpose flour

½ cup sugar

For the topping:

4 eggs

1½ cups sugar

2 tablespoons all-purpose flour

2 tablespoons unsalted butter, melted

Juice and zest from 2 medium lemons

1. To make the crust: Preheat the oven to 350°F. Use a fork or pastry blender to combine the butter, flour, and sugar until the mixture resembles small crumbs. Dump the mixture into a 9-by-13-inch baking dish and press evenly into a crust. Bake for about 15 minutes, or until golden.

2. To make the topping: While the crust is baking, beat the eggs until well blended. Add the sugar, flour, and melted butter. Whisk until well blended. Add the lemon juice and zest and mix well.

3. Pour the mixture onto the warm crust and bake for another 20 to 30 minutes, until the edges are light golden brown. Cool completely before cutting into bars. Dust with powdered sugar (if desired).

EASY CLASSIC
NUT-FREE
VEGETARIAN

YIELDS **24 BARS**

Per Serving

Calories: 159; Total Fat: 6g; Saturated Fat: 3g; Carbohydrates: 26g; Fiber: 1g; Protein: 2g

Tip:

★ Dip a knife in hot water to make cleaner cuts when dividing up bars.

Mango Rice Pudding

PREP TIME: 10 MINUTES / COOK TIME: 30 MINUTES

Using coconut sugar in this recipe enhances the tropical mango flavor.

2 cups water

2 cups instant white jasmine rice (see Tips if not using instant rice)

3 tablespoons unsalted butter, divided

½ cup plus 1 tablespoon coconut sugar

1 teaspoon ground cinnamon, divided

1 mango, peeled and diced (or 3 fresh peaches)

1 cup milk

1. Bring the water to a boil in a heavy saucepan over medium-high heat; stir in the instant rice. Cover and remove from heat. Fluff the rice after 5 minutes.

2. In a skillet over medium heat, melt 2 tablespoons butter with 1 tablespoon coconut sugar and ½ teaspoon cinnamon. Add the mango and cook for 5 minutes, stirring occasionally, until caramelized. Remove from heat.

3. Return the rice to the burner and stir in the milk, remaining coconut sugar, half the cooked mango, remaining butter, and remaining cinnamon. Cook on low for 10 to 15 minutes, until most liquid is absorbed.

4. To serve, spoon the rice pudding into dessert bowls and top each with a tablespoon of caramelized mango. This dish is best served warm.

EASY CLASSIC NUT-FREE VEGETARIAN

SERVES: 6

Per Serving

Calories: 391; Total Fat: 8g; Saturated Fat: 4g; Carbohydrates: 78g; Fiber: 3g; Protein: 6g

Tips:

★ To dice a mango, slice off each side just past the seed. Take each piece and make slices in the flesh without breaking the skin. Scoop out the mango slices with a large spoon, then dice into cubes.

★ If you're using regular jasmine rice, reduce amount to 1 cup and cook in 2 cups of gently boiling water for 20 minutes until liquid is absorbed.

Classic Vanilla Pound Cake

PREP TIME: 15 MINUTES / COOK TIME: 45 MINUTES / COOL TIME: 30 MINUTES

This dense cake is not overly sweet, and it's extremely tasty served with a cup of coffee, fresh fruit and whipped cream, or a scoop of ice cream and chocolate sauce.

2 cups all-purpose flour

1 teaspoon baking powder

½ teaspoon salt

1 cup butter, softened

1⅔ cups sugar

5 eggs, room temperature

1 teaspoon almond extract

1 teaspoon vanilla extract

1. Preheat the oven to 350°F. Grease and flour a 10-cup Bundt pan.

2. Sift the flour, baking powder, and salt into a bowl.

3. Using a stand mixer with a paddle attachment, cream the butter for 2 to 3 minutes, until it is lighter in color. Add the sugar and mix for 2 more minutes, until light and fluffy.

4. Add the eggs one at a time, beating just until the yolks disappear after each addition. Stir in the almond extract and vanilla extract.

5. Gently add the flour to the wet mixture, mixing on low speed until incorporated.

6. Pour the batter into the pan and bake for 45 to 50 minutes, or until a toothpick comes out clean.

7. Cool the cake in the pan on a wire rack for 30 minutes before inverting onto to a cake plate. Dust with powdered sugar (if desired).

EASY CLASSIC
NUT-FREE
VEGETARIAN

SERVES: **12**

Per Serving

Calories: 352; Total Fat: 17g; Saturated Fat: 10g; Carbohydrates: 46g; Fiber: 1g; Protein: 5g

Tips:

* The most accurate way to measure flour for baking is to spoon it into a measuring cup until full, then level off with the back of a knife.

* To freeze, let it cool completely, then wrap in a couple layers of plastic wrap and a couple layers of aluminum foil. Store in the freezer for up to 3 months. To thaw, remove the wrapping and let stand at room temperature for 2 to 3 hours.

Rustic Apple Tart

Rustic fruit tarts are open-faced pies with a free form crust. This recipe is a great use for my No-Fail Pie Crust. A very forgiving pie for the novice baker, this fall dessert is delicious served with a dollop of fresh whipped cream.

1 No-Fail Pie Crust (see page 143)

3½ tablespoons sugar, divided

1 tablespoon all-purpose flour

4 large apples peeled, cored and cut into ¼-inch-thick slices

2 tablespoons butter, melted

2 tablespoons apricot preserves, melted

1. Preheat the oven to 400°F.

2. On a lightly floured surface, roll the pie crust into a 16-inch circle.

3. Line a large rimmed baking sheet with parchment paper. Roll dough around a rolling pin and unroll it onto the prepared baking sheet.

4. Mix together 2 tablespoons sugar and the flour, and sprinkle over the dough. Arrange the apple slices on top in overlapping circles, leaving a 3-inch edge to fold over the apples.

5. Brush the melted butter on top of the apples and sprinkle with the remaining sugar.

6. Refrigerate for 10 minutes, then bake for about 1 hour, or until the apples are tender and the crust is golden.

7. Brush the apples with the melted apricot preserves. Cool slightly before serving.

REINVENTION
NUT-FREE
VEGETARIAN

SERVES: **10**

Per Serving

Calories: 158; Total Fat: 7g; Saturated Fat: 2g; Carbohydrates: 25g; Fiber: 3g; Protein: 1g

Flavor Swap:

* For a fresh summertime pie, substitute sliced peaches for the apples.

Fruit Pizza

This unconventional recipe is almost as fun to make as it is to eat.

1 batch Frozen Sugar Cookie Dough, thawed (see page 144)

1 (8-ounce) package cream cheese, softened

½ cup sugar

1 teaspoon vanilla extract

2 ½ cups fresh berries (if using strawberries, hulled and sliced)

¼ cup apricot preserves, melted, optional

1. Preheat the oven to 350°F. Evenly press enough cookie dough into a pizza pan for ⅛-inch thickness; bake for 8 to 10 minutes until golden. Remove from the oven and cool completely.

2. Use an electric mixer to beat the cream cheese, sugar, and vanilla extract until smooth. Spread over the cooled cookie crust.

3. Top the pizza with fresh berries. Just before serving, lightly brush the fruit with the melted apricot preserves (if desired).

REINVENTION
NUT-FREE
VEGETARIAN

SERVES: **12**

Per Serving

Calories: 288; Total Fat: 15g; Saturated Fat: 6g; Carbohydrates: 28g; Fiber: 3g; Protein: 1g

Tips:

★ You can use store-bought frozen cookie dough If you didn't have time to make your own.

★ Dip your fingers in flour to avoid getting them too sticky when pressing the cookie dough into the pan.

★ You can assemble and refrigerate the fruit pizza ahead of time if needed, but, for the best results, don't brush with the preserves until you're ready to serve it.

Balsamic Strawberry Parfaits

PREP TIME: 15 MINUTES / CHILL TIME: 30 MINUTES

Macerating strawberries in balsamic vinegar and honey instead of refined sugar makes these parfaits a bit more wholesome.

1½ tablespoons honey

2 teaspoons traditional aged balsamic vinegar

1 pint fresh strawberries, hulled and sliced

1 cup Coconut Granola (see page 26)

2 cups vanilla Greek yogurt

1. Mix together the honey and balsamic vinegar. Pour the mixture over the sliced strawberries and toss gently to coat. Refrigerate for 30 minutes.

2. Spoon 1 tablespoon of granola into the bottom of 4 tall dessert glasses. Top each with 2 tablespoons of Greek yogurt, then 1 tablespoon of the strawberry mixture. Repeat the layers until the glasses are full. Drizzle with additional honey or balsamic vinegar (if desired), and serve.

REINVENTION
VEGETARIAN

SERVES: **4**

Per Serving

Calories: 270; Total Fat: 6g;
Saturated Fat: 3g;
Carbohydrates: 47g;
Fiber: 4g; Protein: 11g

Chocolate Bread Pudding

PREP TIME: 15 MINUTES / COOK TIME: 45 MINUTES

Its delicious indulgence aside, I love how easily this dessert can be assembled and baked as you enjoy dinner with your friends. Serve it hot out of the oven with even more of my Boozy Chocolate Sauce, and be ready for the satisfying sighs from your guests to follow.

Butter, for greasing

½ loaf challah (or brioche), cut into 2-inch cubes (about 6 cups)

⅓ cup sugar

¾ cup Boozy Chocolate Sauce (see page 142), divided

3 cups milk

3 eggs, beaten

1 teaspoon vanilla extract

Pinch salt

1. Preheat the oven to 350°F. Use the butter to grease bottom and sides of an 11-by-7-inch baking dish. Add the challah cubes, sprinkle with sugar, and drizzle ¼ cup Boozy Chocolate Sauce on top.

2. Whisk together the milk, eggs, and vanilla extract. Pour the mixture over the bread and let soak for 15 minutes.

3. Bake for 45 to 50 minutes, or until custard is set and edges of bread have browned. Remove and drizzle with about ¼ cup Boozy Chocolate Sauce.

4. Serve warm or at room temperature. Drizzle each serving with another tablespoon of Boozy Chocolate Sauce (if desired).

REINVENTION
NUT-FREE
VEGETARIAN

SERVES: **6 TO 8**

Per Serving

Calories: 387; Total Fat: 15g; Saturated Fat: 4g; Carbohydrates: 53g; Fiber: 1g; Protein: 11g

Tip:

* If you're making this dessert for a dinner party, cube the bread ahead of time, then place it in the baking dish and sprinkle it with sugar. Just before you sit down to dinner, follow the remaining recipe instructions and let the bread pudding bake while you enjoy your meal.

The Dirty Dozen™ &
The Clean Fifteen™

A nonprofit environmental watchdog organization called Environmental Working Group (EWG) looks at data supplied by the US Department of Agriculture (USDA) and the Food and Drug Administration (FDA) about pesticide residues. Each year it compiles a list of the best and worst pesticide loads found in commercial crops. You can use these lists to decide which fruits and vegetables to buy organic to minimize your exposure to pesticides and which produce is considered safe enough to buy conventionally. This does not mean they are pesticide-free, though, so wash these fruits and vegetables thoroughly. The list is updated annually, and you can find it online at EWG.org/FoodNews.

The Dirty Dozen™

1. strawberries
2. spinach
3. kale
4. nectarines
5. apples
6. grapes
7. peaches
8. cherries
9. pears
10. tomatoes
11. celery
12. potatoes

Additionally, nearly three-quarters of hot pepper samples contained pesticide residues.

The Clean Fifteen™

1. avocados
2. sweet corn
3. pineapples
4. sweet peas (frozen)
5. onions
6. papayas
7. eggplants
8. asparagus
9. kiwis
10. cabbages
11. cauliflower
12. cantaloupes
13. broccoli
14. mushrooms
15. honeydew melons

Measurement Conversions

Oven Temperatures

Fahrenheit (F)	Celsius (C) (approx.)
250°F	120°C
300°F	150°C
325°F	165°C
350°F	180°C
375°F	190°C
400°F	200°C
425°F	220°C
450°F	230°C

Volume Equivalents (Liquid)

US Standard	US Standard (oz.)	Metric (approx.)
2 tablespoons	1 fl. oz.	30 mL
¼ cup	2 fl. oz.	60 mL
½ cup	4 fl. oz.	120 mL
1 cup	8 fl. oz.	240 mL
1½ cups	12 fl. oz.	355 mL
2 cups or 1 pint	16 fl. oz.	475 mL
4 cups or 1 quart	32 fl. oz.	1 L
1 gallon	128 fl. oz.	4 L

Weight Equivalents

US Standard	Metric (approx.)
½ ounce	15 g
1 ounce	30 g
2 ounces	60 g
4 ounces	115 g
8 ounces	225 g
12 ounces	340 g
16 ounces or 1 pound	455 g

Volume Equivalents (Dry)

US Standard	Metric (approx.)
⅛ teaspoon	0.5 mL
¼ teaspoon	1 mL
½ teaspoon	2 mL
¾ teaspoon	4 mL
1 teaspoon	5 mL
1 tablespoon	15 mL
¼ cup	59 mL
⅓ cup	79 mL
½ cup	118 mL
⅔ cup	156 mL
¾ cup	177 mL
1 cup	235 mL
2 cups or 1 pint	475 mL
3 cups	700 mL
4 cups or 1 quart	1 L

Resources

LifeLoveAndGoodFood.com—This is my own blog, where you'll find many quick and easy recipes using fresh and wholesome ingredients.

Farm-to-doorstep delivery services rescue produce that would otherwise go to waste due to overproduction or imperfections. These perfectly healthy groceries are typically sold for much less than the produce on your grocery store shelves:

* ImperfectProduce.com—Subscription boxes available for delivery in many major cities across the United States. Check the website to see if delivery is available in your area.
* HungryHarvest.com—Subscription boxes available for delivery in Maryland, Washington, D.C., Virginia, greater Philadelphia, southern New Jersey, northern Delaware, south Florida, The Triangle Area and Charlotte in North Carolina, and the Detroit metro area.

You may find one of these smartphone shopping list apps helpful:

* Our Groceries—This customizable shopping list is grouped in your most-used categories and can be instantly synchronized to all the smart phones in your household. You can also add items to the list using any Alexa-enabled device.
* Out of Milk—Create and share shopping lists or use one of the pre-made grocery list templates. This app includes an essential household supplies list for kitchen, bathroom, and laundry and is compatible with Alexa as well.

Online grocery shopping options:

* Major grocery store chains—Visit your grocery store's website to check if they offer online shopping. One bonus to this is that most allow you to order items you've previously purchased by serving them up on your home page after logging in.

* Amazon Fresh—Amazon offers Whole Foods brands at cheaper prices and lets you subscribe for delivery of repeat items you use most often, like coffee, for instance. Amazon Prime members are given a free trial and then charged a monthly fee for unlimited deliveries with a minimum order.
* Instacart and Google Express—These services source from many stores and then compiles the order into one delivery. Some store options include Whole foods, Costco, drug stores, and pet supply stores. Check first to see whether each store requires a minimum order.

Recipe Type Index

Index

Acknowledgments

To my husband and best friend, John: Thank you. I could never express my full gratitude for the way you always believe in me and encourage me without fail. I love you forever.

To Allison and Lindsay: Being your mother is my greatest joy. I am so proud of the confident, compassionate women you've become and feel blessed to have adult children whom I also consider my sweet friends. I love you, girls.

To the memory of Lillian Lee Clemmons Burkhart: Thank you for giving me basic cooking lessons and adopting me into the Burkhart family. You took me under your wing and loved me as your own granddaughter. The years you lived with us on the farm and the fun we had together will never be forgotten.

About the Author

Sheila Thigpen, creator of the blog, *Life, Love, and Good Food* (lifeloveandgoodfood.com), spent more than twenty years as a business manager in the publishing industry, overseeing creative teams and projects for many national brands. She retired in 2018 to focus on her passions: creating and sharing good food, photography, and blogging.

A graduate of the University of Tennessee with a degree in journalism, she launched her blog in 2014 as an outlet for her own creativity. Her popular, growing, food blog inspires home chefs to spend more time in the kitchen—and around the family dinner table—with quick and easy recipes, beautiful photography, clear instructions, and tips for cooking success.

She is a born-and-raised Southern girl now living in Knoxville, Tennessee, near the beautiful Smoky Mountains. She and her husband have two adult daughters, are active in their church, love to travel, and are still over-the-moon excited about becoming grandparents last year.

CPSIA information can be obtained
at www.ICGtesting.com
Printed in the USA
JSHW020939201119
2523JS00002B/2